Can You Let Go?

Ed Rychkun

There is no copyright to this book. If it helps you to understand life, create a better one and learn to develop your own miracles, go ahead and copy whatever you need.

www.edrychkun.com

ISBN 978-0-9810702-6-1

ALL THERE IS IS LOVE

All there is, is Light and Love
Our Hearts an expression of One above
For here is where the light can shine
To choose of fear or the Divine
Its presence doth govern a heaven or hell
It's the way of it we can all foretell
For darkness comes when light dims
A choice we alone make through our whims
Within you lies a curious device
That turns a dimmer to a choice
Withdraw the light and pull love away
Or shine the light to make it stay
Whatever choice is up to you
But know your life will so ensue
What is this curious device you say?
It is your mind and beliefs that weigh
Upon the way you view your life
One of bliss one of strife
It is your Higher Mind that knows
How to make that heart glow
And leave the Lower Mind behind
It's true self through ego hard to find
So turn the switch to full I say
Live in bliss each moment each day
Shine the light on all that exists
For it's me as One with all that is

CONTENTS

What you read and find in this book
May open your beliefs with a new look
And if your heart it does awaken
Don't be surprised if ego is shaken

SCHMIRACLES | MIRACLES
MANIFESTING | CO-CREATION
HOLLOW PHYSICS | HOLOGRAPHIC
HOLD ON | LET GO
OUTSIDE | INSIDE
NOTHING | EVERYTHING
HOLOGRAMS | REALITY
LOWER | HIGHER
RULES | COVENANTS
PRACTICE | REALITY
BEFORE | AFTER
MAN | GOD
END | BEGIN

You will find it is your own belief
That may indeed have been the thief
That limits you from finding you
And knowing what is really true

SCHMIRACLE | MIRACLE

It's all in the mind I hear them say
But what's this disease I have today?
If miracles are real and they are true
Then why can't I have a miracle too?

There is an instant in time where some people go through a paradigm shift in their life. The most common occurrence of this is when they are subjected to a healing miracle and suddenly life is not the same—everything changes. Others have a Near Death or Out of Body experience and when they come back from their little vacation in the cosmos, everything changes—attitudes, beliefs, habits, and purpose. Their whole way of life takes on a new meaning. Yes, what may have been *schmiracle* pooh-poohing changes to *miracle* woo wooing as within an instant in time behavior and beliefs shift.

In most cases there is an abrupt change to a place where perceptions, attitudes, actions seem to be "higher" because something miraculous happens. In the case of a healing miracle, not only is there some unexplainable instant physical change, something changes in the "vibration" or "resonating frequency" of the human essence. The mind shift that takes place appears to be from a lower plane to an upper of the belief system which then congeals into new behavior and a new conscious awareness.

The physical shift is the incredible healing that occurs. The mind shift is typically to a more spiritual consciousness. Why does this mind shift happen in some? What is it that attracts the physical change? What causes the mind to let go of the old ways and take on the new? What causes the mind to then translate this shift into a new way of life with a new purpose? Clearly it has to be about *letting go* of something that occurs in the mind, triggered by the body change—the miracle. How can this happen? If you have ever met, or read about these thousands and thousands of cases, you will quickly understand these people cannot be convinced by any scientific genius that it did not happen. And there *ain't* no way you cannot see a dramatic change—to the better I might add. It is a totally unscientific, unpredictable process of shifting into a totally different reality. Yet it happens all over the planet.

Healing miracles and Near Death Experiences are indeed wondrous examples of this peculiar shift in the body and mind. In most cases, this shift is facilitated by some event, person, or situation that is created as the experience. It could be a ceremony, a ritual, a process, a pill, an object, a morphic field or even the mind itself. Whatever it is, it is the mind and its belief that is the common denominator. It has to be convinced or it has to be receptive before anything happens. Perhaps the most dramatic example of this paradigm mind/body shift in action is the placebo effect.

A very famous case was reported by Bruno Klopfer[1], a psychologist who was treating a man named Wright for advanced cancer. Bedridden in the hospital, Wright needed an oxygen mask to survive. Diagnosed with a few days left to live, this man was filled with tumors of the lymph nodes the size of oranges. All hope of *any* recovery was exhausted. But Wright did not want to die.

---

[1] www.what-is-cancer.com/papers/newmedicine/placeboandcancer.html

He heard about Krebiozen, a new drug that was available for trial. Of course this was a waste of time to the doctor but with Wright's persistence, he finally gave in and the drug was administered to Wright on a Friday.

On Monday, when the Doc came in, he found Wright out of bed walking around. Inspections indicated his tumors had melted like snowballs on a hot stove. Ten days later, Wright left the hospital cancer free.

Wright was active for about two months until he read some articles stating that Kreibozen actually had no affect on cancer of the lymph nodes. Being very logical and scientific, Wright suffered a relapse and was readmitted to the hospital. The tumors were back, as were lung issues that required oxygen; it was all the same again.

Quite perplexed about this strange and dramatic shifting, the Doc decided to try something like a placebo. In this experiment he told Wright Kreibozen was actually effective and that the problem was some of the initial supplies had deteriorated during shipping. He said he had a new concentrated version and did Wright want to try it. The Doc had a plan to inject Wright with a plain water placebo but with the usual ceremony.

Again within days, the tumors melted, the chest fluid vanished and Wright was back on his feet feeling great. This went on for two months. Then Wright found out the American Medical Association announced that the nationwide study of Kreibozen had found the drug useless in treating cancer. Wright's cancer instantly blossomed and he died two days later.

What's happening here? Makes you think doesn't it? First, what does any pill really do? Secondly, what powers do your doctor's statements have over you? Third, what power does your mind actually have that you are not aware of? So is there any reason why anybody can't create an endless supply of placebo pills? Of course not, maybe they already are and it is the marketing hype and your Doc that convince you. Will they work? Not all the time. Why not? Well, do *you* believe they will? Yes, indeed, it is the magic question.

Why do I present this special case? There are actually millions of these unexplained cases, some even more dramatic. I bring these forward into your awareness because sometimes it is the trigger that shifts belief. Did you believe any of it, or did you look immediately for reasons that it could be some fake? These dramatic cases are documented, observed facts that give you a glimpse into what is a possibility that you may have never even considered. If you start looking and opening your awareness, the staggering truth of it is that these many cases are not isolated; there are thousands more. None can be explained but they nevertheless exist. You have simply been conditioned to believe they are some sort of anomaly that is interesting and perhaps entertaining but of no relevance in your life. Right? Did you?

The first very important thing to understand here is that these physical anomalies like miracles and materialization do exist. Simply because they cannot be explained does not discredit them from existence. Secondly, how can you ever assume that you yourself cannot benefit from such an experience, or even do it yourself? Moreover, what makes you think that it can't happen again, and again, and to you? Yes, to you? Yes, let go of the beliefs that create the limits.

Belief may be the thief to health

Have you ever considered that your mind, with attention to your issues of dis-ease and disease, and dysfunction may be the main culprit holding onto your health issues?

The placebo conundrum with Wright is not the only example of how a belief in the Doctor or the remedy can work miracles. My quest has been to pursue the answers to the question of how this happens and why not me. Why am I burdened with health issues? Being an analytical type there had to be some way I could figure this out.

My conundrum became like that of the quantum physicist trying to understand how consciousness—some invisible force of nothing—plays such a significant part in material physics. They can't. The answers do not slumber in science. How can they? Science sets the rules of behavior based on observation. And today's science was yesterday's science fiction. Like the invisible force of consciousness as a major component of quantum physics, I ran into these other invisible forces reflected by things like belief, trust, surrender, faith, and letting go. These seemed to always be part of the miracle process. Although only concepts of some invisible energy, they were like a brick wall that prevented any degree of new beliefs to be formed. Worst of all I had no reference as to what the words really meant to me.

In my last book, **Miracle, Miracle I Wish to Find Where you Hide Within My Mind,** I brought to light the methods of some of the best Miracle Workers and Healers that create wondrous, unexplainable miracles all the time. Not only did I study their works, I took some of their training courses to see them in action. I seemed to always encounter faith—faith that a healing would be done by some one or some thing. In addition, I have personal friends who are Energy Healers with many profound healing examples. They insist they are not healers; they only facilitate the healing process. So what is it they facilitate? They don't heal any more that a doctor does. What is it that takes on the chore of the actually healing?

Wright simply believed that the treatment and his doctor would solve his problems, even though they were both total fakers. Wright invoked something though his belief that responded almost instantly. The Doc and his ritual of injection, plus the BS about the drug facilitated a healing. Wright simply had the faith in them and the drug that this would be so. And when that faith was lost, guess what? It was all undone as rapidly. Physical matter shifted into a different form. In truth, none of the Doc, the drug, the ritual could be the ones that healed Wright directly, could they?

And yet, if this trickery had been performed on other cases of similar nature, it may have never produced the same results. What was different about Wright's faith?

I never paid much attention to that word faith because it seemed to be linked with religious beliefs many of which were pretty dogmatic to me. Upon looking more closely at this word, I found that faith is the confident belief or trust in the truth or trustworthiness of a person, idea, or thing. The dictionary says the word faith is typically used to refer to a religion itself or to religion in general. And when surrounded with trust, faith involves a concept of events or outcomes. Almost universally it refers to a trusting belief in a transcendent reality, or else in a Supreme Being and/or this being's role in the order of transcendent, spiritual things. But it is also used conversely for a belief not resting on logical proof or material evidence. Hmmm. So what? Did this mean I had to have faith that a miracle would occur? That seemed pretty easy!

Well, it seems that faith has to refer to my faith—my personal belief—whatever that may be. I had to have faith strong enough to persuade the mind that a certain statement is true. Belief had to really believe this and agree with the mind as to the truth of what was declared, and believe that the Big Guy in the sky or *someone* would do the healing job at hand. So you convince yourself to simply trust something is true and surrender to this—let go of any other's belief or truth that may interfere with this truth. But what did I need to have this *faith in* to support the belief? What or who actually did the healing? Was it the mind? Was it a Supreme Power, God, what?

What I found was that for those who are used to creating healing miracles, they have a solid faith indeed that it will be done. But not all their healings work all the time. But what was interesting was that they did put faith in something, whether you call this a Supreme Being, whether it is God, Consciousness, The Force, The Divine, The Heart, The Creator, or whatever. And the other thing that popped out is they engaged the heart. How? It was by being empathic to a cause, to a betterment of the individual, to a feeling of emotion of peace and love. That was their way of **"going into the heart"**. It was within this ritual or morphic field that something was simply trusted to take place. And in many cases, it does! What *is relevant* is that there is some indescribable, awesome universal power that assists in the process some of the time.

What about Wright? What did he do after the Doc facilitated the ritual? The mind and a Higher Power had to be the healers. In this case the Higher Power may have been the Doc but he didn't even believe it would work. And as I said, if you had five patients like Mr. Wright, the placebo would work on maybe only a few—or even none at all.

As I described in the book, it became obvious that all these techniques and success stories had some common elements. These brought some rather unscientific and loosey goosey terms into the forefront. Successful healing miracles were always based on some of these other words besides belief, faith and trust. These came up all the time, like surrender, love, and compassion. They engaged in the actions of intention, attention, unconditional, going within, and being in the heart. They all vibrated with the energy of letting go of our outside material reality and dropping into a different imaginary reality that drew the miracle process to the patient even when the patient apparently did nothing at all.

Some healers used devices, crystals, special energy devices—a huge deluge of Newageceuticals and Energyceuticals. And some worked, _some of the time_. I did not really get it. I battled with understanding the meaning of those words. But what kept ringing was if they can do it, why can't I? What am I missing?

What these were inferring was that **YOU** had to believe in something or someone that could fix you. You had to surrender to them or it and let go of anything that was limiting you in your thinking that brought doubt into the process. Then you would let some power loose. Then keep the faith and trust that it would happen. Then you were ripe for the performance.

But how do you surrender? Traditionally, many have not had a problem doing this. We have _surrendered_ to others all the time. Whether it is the advice of your doctor, the experts, your tax accountant, the government, marketing hype, or whatever, it doesn't matter. You have placed your _faith and trust_ in someone else or something and _let go_ of dealing with it yourself. You accept the advice and it is your belief that they will help you. Clearly there is some mindset that forms as a strong belief and you let go of any limits and opinions.

So in regards to healing miracles, something happens when you do this surrender and faith thing. To me it still was not clear who the real healer was. And why did all these miracle makers engage the heart? It was about going inside—to the heart.

In my research, I was beginning to form a new model of the Greater Power. It indeed had to do with the heart. But why not *go inside* to the liver, or the pancreas? What was so special about a heart? Well, I have to say this answer came at first from the volumes of work done by a group called HeartMath[2]. This group has shown that the physical heart has its own neural network like the brain. It also can control the body functions. And it has a stronger energy field, shaped like a torus, larger than any other field of the body. This is the center of the strongest and possibly the most influential energy system we have.

So why go to the heart? It is the center of the Divine Power—you. Over and over, I would end up at the same place. This was a place that was linked directly to the Higher Mind—a place where the Divine Heart—the invisible energy field surrounding the physical organ resided. That's why we don't go to the liver or pancreas. These are the two energy systems that you surrender your thinking to and have the faith and trust that they will guide you and help you with a miracle through your life instead of your normal mind. It means letting go and *going inside* to join up with heart. The big question is why and how?

Over and over, I got to the vague expressions of "*go inside, go to the heart, create attention and intent, surrender, detach from the outcome, zero out your intellect, get the emotional body vibrating with desire, show faith and trust, and be thankful for the solution?*

How, I would ask. What do I do? How do I know that I am doing the right thing? Well, the vague answer from the real miracle makers was: "*Do it anyway you like to*

---

[2] www.heartmath.org

deploy those words but just do it and believe in whatever you decide they mean."

In the Miracle, Miracle book, I offered some trite suggestions on how to execute the paradigm shift on *doing the right thing*:

You*: "How do you know this is right?"*
Me: "*I just do*."
You: *"How do you create the right attention?"*
Me: *"By bringing something into your mind."*
You: *"How do you go inside to the Heart?"*
Me: *"Anyway you like or just say it to be so."*
You: *"How do you detach from the outcome?"*
Me: *"Stop thinking."*
You: *"How do you zero out your intellect?"*
Me: *"Trust there is guidance from the heart."*
You: *"How do you vibrate with desire?"*
Me: *"Feel the bliss of being perfect."*
You: *"How do you believe without doubt?"*
Me: *"Because it simply is."*
You: *"Is there a specific procedure?"*
Me: *"No, it is what works for you."*
You: *"So how do you know you are doing it properly?"*
Me: *"When it works."*
You: *"Well how long will that take?"*
Me: "*As long as you take."*
You: *"Anything else?"*
Me: "*Yes, use the words I love you a lot!"*

No, it does not satisfy the question of how, does it? It is because the big variable that controls when and how is belief and faith!

But what it highlights is that there is a process in creating healing miracles that has to be uniquely yours, formed in your own belief system, and that this engages the heart as your helper. It suggests that you have to let go of preconceived limits and replace these with some unyielding knowing that if you surrender to a buddy called the Heart, things will happen. I have hopefully opened you to your best buddy when you want to have your own healing miracles happen. But now I want to cover the other part of changing your life to do with wealth and material miracles.

> **Miracle, Miracle, how do I find**
> **Where you hide within my mind?**
> **It's your belief it said to me**
> **Ask your heart to set them free**

MANIFESTING | CO-CREATION

Invoke your intent and what you feel
Make that desire oh so real
Invoke the heart with Divine appeal
And so it swiftly does congeal

I am going to shift into another topic that deals with the abundance area of manifesting. It is all about awareness to, and management of, your personal energy. If you knew without doubt that what you thought and felt created the kind of life you have, would you think differently?

First, let me tell you about an incredible example that distorts the physical beliefs of science. It has to do with materialization—creating an object instantly out of thin air. The most famous modern day materializer and miracle maker is **Sathya Sai Baba** an Indian Holy man in Southern India. He is reported to materialize lockets, rings, jewelry, delicacies, sacred ash, and specific objects that are requested by others. He creates these out of thin air then passes them out as gifts. Thousands have witnessed this. Scientists who study this are befuddled by it of course, simply discounting it and claiming it is a hoax.

In his book ***Modern Miracles: An Investigative Report on Psychic Phenomonena Associated with Sathya Sai Baba***, author and researcher ***Erlendur***

Haraldsson[3] presents his work on this man who truly boggles the mind. He, a Professor of Psychology at the University of Iceland, set out to research this strange phenomenon and report his findings.

When interviewed, Sai Baba insisted: *"Daily and spiritual life must grow together."* He is deemed a saint, and he is visited by many daily to materialize vast quantities of food; even sizzling hot delicacies fall from his hands and feet. He can produce exotic and rare objects, fruits, and even anomalous ones like half apple, half orange on two sides. He walks about producing sacred ash with the wave of his hands. Haraldsson reports these have been observed and filmed endlessly. He states it is not mass hypnosis and Sai Baba has been doing this since the age of 14. He produces things from nothing using the attention of his mind. No one has ever been able to discredit him. The reference is below so check this out for yourself.

Sai Baba is also a biolocation example. Numerous witnesses report watching him snap his fingers and vanish instantly reappearing several hundred feet away.

This is not an isolated case. There are many Holy men in India with this ability. In the book, **Autobiography of a Yogi, Paramahansa Yogananada**, the first eminent holy man of India is reported to materialize out-of-season fruits, gold plates and other objects. He said: *"The world is nothing but an objectivized dream and whatever your powerful mind believes very intensely instantly comes to pass."*

In his book **Human Levitation**, **Preston Dennett**, tells us there are over 330 cases of levitation reported. Many have been photographed and scientists who study this have only received heartburn and headaches trying to

---

[3] http://www.saibabaofindia.com/sai_baba_haraldsson.html

explain it. They can't, so they deem it a hoax and ignore it.

Miracles of attraction and manifesting

Like many, I was initially captivated by the deluge of material and mania on the Law of Attraction. It promised the big "Secret" to manifesting your dreams and it was certainly good marketing. But it was not long before I realized there was a lot missing from this marketing hype. It sounded like I could have everything through this law that everybody forgot about. Well, the number of blogs from people who clearly *did not get* the million dollars or find the genie, reflect a frustration that sometimes it works but not always. What was even more un-nerving was that the people preaching the law did not seem to be the results of, nor the beneficiaries of, their attracted abundance and miracles. But like miracles themselves, success came some of the time to some. The great news was that it was at least getting people to pay more attention to the way they think.

I am a believer in the Law of Attraction. I could myself expound on it and its workings as a cosmic law of energy but there was still something eluding me because abundance was not flowing so freely. There was something missing. As the quest continued, I began to find answers from a place that I never would have expected—from the heart.

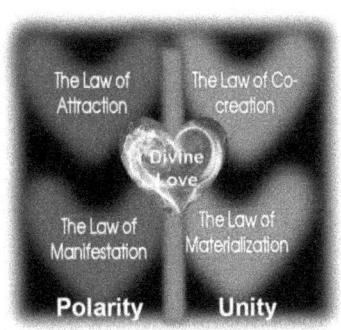

Look at the cover of this book. There is a dividing line between the worlds of Polarity and Unity with a heart in the middle. On the polarity side, we have the Law of Attraction and the Law of Manifestation. On this side the energy you create attracts like energy and is the way to manifest energy proactively. It is based on energy you give life to that follows a cosmic law of finding an energy mate.

On the other side, we have The Law of Co-creation and the Law of Materialization. It is the place where the Miracle workers go for a few moments, and people like Sai Baba go fulltime. Why is there a division at the heart? Because that's where the shift occurs. On one side you simply believe you can't. On the other side you believe you can. On one side you are polarized from the heart and on the other side you are unity with it. What is the significance of the heart? Again, it is the Divine energy center—your co-creating buddy. On the Polarity side you engage the heart through charging your energy with emotions. On the Unity side, the heart is a full time buddy.

But here is the most interesting part. These four laws are the tip of the iceberg. It relates to a word used a lot these days; vibration. I will get to in the next chapter but it is the frequency that your electromagnetic body vibrates at. The emotion of love is a high positive vibration, as are other emotions of the heart. Hate is a low vibration. The vibrational change process starts once you stop "sleeping".

This is the time where the vast majority of humans are simply accepting that they have limited control of their lives and experience whatever karma comes at them. Following is a little picture following of the vibrational evolution that occurs as a human awakens to letting go. Notice the different stages when you stop sleeping; awakening, awakened, expanded, enlightened, ascended. This is the process referred to as Ascension. Notice the dividing line again.

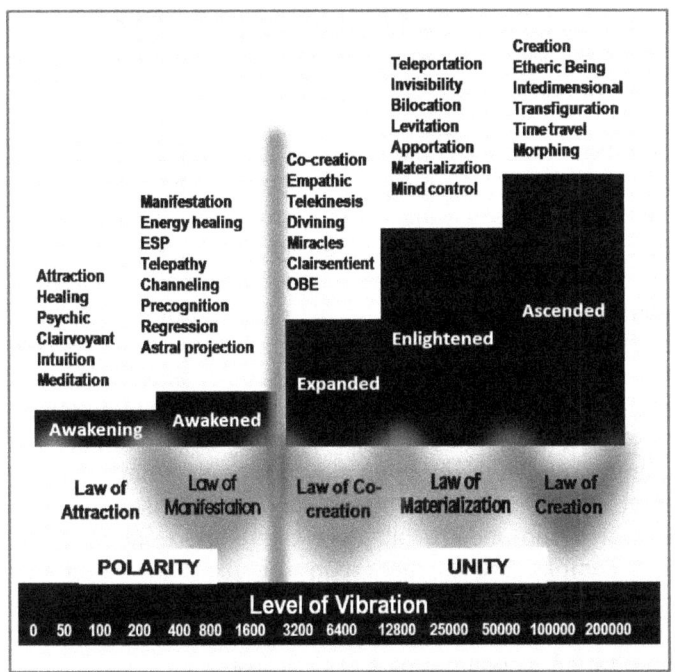

We will come back to this diagram several times but for now think about a simple analogy. Consider how a material object such as ice changes its rate of vibrational frequency and its properties as heat is placed on it. It *sleeps* as ice but starts *awakening* when heat is applied. At the *awakened* stage it becomes water and at the *expanded* stage it is steam. At the *enlightened* stage it is now no thing and at the *ascended* stage it is pure spiritual energy. The evolution brought totally different properties each time as the energy simply changed form evolving back to its original state of no thing. no thing being every-thing or all of creation.

Now consider the power of love of high vibration (like fire) being applied to a human (like ice) that is at a state of lower vibration. This unfolds in a similar evolution with new properties coming out at each stage. The more love (heat) you apply to this body (ice), the more the body, and its properties change in energy form. If you look at some of these properties on the chart, you get the drift of what these properties are.

The first stage after the power of love wakes you is what I refer to as **awakening**. It is when you begin to realize that your mind and body are energy generators (thoughts, images, words, emotions) that give life to energies. You begin to realize that you may be creating your own destiny and reality with these energies because once you give them life, they have a sole function of attracting situations, people, and things that create like experiences. Hence the **Law of Attraction** hits you. You may begin to see that thinking and creating negative energies may not be so smart. So you start to think more about stopping these negative energies and show a bit more tolerance, understanding and compassion. In fact, many people that are at this stage show several metaphysical abilities like healing, psychic, intuition, meditation, clairvoyance, and meditation as being a part of their lives.

The next stage I call the **awakened** stage when you begin to realize that you can proactively control energies, experiences, and perceptions so as to draw to you more of what you desire. This is where you begin to place a conscious awareness on the energies avoiding negative ones and then proactively managing the positive to begin to carve out your life differently. Your attention, perception, and intention, when it comes to creating perceptions, thoughts, emotions, images, and words begins to take on a more love-compassion fundamentalism. It is at this state that you are working on the **Law of Manifestation** and typically you find people with new properties (abilities) like energy healing, ESP, telepathy, channeling, precognition, regression, and astral projection to name a few. Here you are now engaging the heart through feelings and emotions.

As the next stage is reached which I call **expanded**, something changes dramatically. This is where the big wall is broken down and instead of attracting and manifesting with existing energy matter to bring experiences; you begin to defy the laws of classical physics to actually create new outcomes of matter. Yes, it is where you *Let Go.* The best example of this is a healing miracle brought about by energy healers, placebos and other miraculous recoveries where suddenly, in an instant in time, a situation—like a broken bone—corrects itself.

This stage is attained when you realize that if you solicit the assistance of a new Divine buddy—your Co-creator Heart—letting go of classical beliefs and surrendering to it, you can do things that are deemed impossible by science. Yes, the **Law of Co-creation** sits here. Here you find empathics, telepathics, telekinesis, diviners, out of bodiers, clairsentience, miracle healers, diviners, clairvoyants, and so on. These are some of the new abilities that open to those that have learned to let go and trust the co-creator partner will assist. What is important here is that there is a realization of being in the heart to truly open these new abilities. This is the shift away from Polarity where you believed you were separate from the Divine goes to that of belief in Unity. This is a place where you and the Divine are One. Yes, the heart is your personal link to your Higher Divine Self.

The next stage **enlightened** really gets serious. When the attitude is totally One and you are full time in the heart. It means total empathy for all things. Here the belief is we are interconnected and to affect anything else affects us and visa versa. This is where Sai Baba sits. Teleportation, materialization, levitation, apportation, mind control, bilocation and invisibility are a few of the characteristics here. This is where that Co-creator partner is being employed full time. This is where the **Law of Materialization** becomes a reality. The laws of classical physics simply don't apply here as the traditional laws of material, gravity, and solids get violated. This stage occurs when you learn to really let go most of the time. You live "in your heart". You are a complete empath showing heightened, unconditional love and compassion—those high vibration fires—for all things as they are you. You now firmly hand command to the Higher Divine Mind that you have replaced with your material limits and ego driven existence. And you have absolute faith and trust in this Higher Self of mind and body.

The next stage is **ascended**. You have become aware and know without the slightest doubt that you are an interdimensional, etheric Being of Light, borrowing a body temporarily to expand the universe. You are here to express your Higher and Lower Self through the hologram you created on this planet. You are able to move interdimensionally. Your life is total compassion, service and love. Nothing else exists to you, and if it does, it is there for you to simply transcend it to the light.

This may seem a bit heavy, but I have to assume you are not sleeping anymore and that is why you are reading this book. But there is no reason except that which is in your own mind all as to why you cannot deploy these laws properly in your life, and there is no reason at all why you cannot experience a miracle, or even create one yourself. It is about first emptying your mind by letting go of the old so the new stuff can enter. How else can new possibilities come into your life?

Perhaps you may be thinking that many of these "gifts" and "talents" which smell of metaphysical are of no interest to you. Perhaps that is why you are still Sleeping? Well as you sleep, your laws of attraction and manifestation are having a great party doing their own thing under the control of the ego. Well be aware ego is there to protect you and to it the body is expendable. It likes to create fear of past and future because it likes to remind you of what nasty thing others did to you and how you must prepare for your future. Be aware that fear, opposite of love as the same strength. So you manifest things the same way, attracting what you create. The big difference is that the heart does not engage in this, translating its unease into the physical by creating disease, then diseases (like hypertension and heart disease) into the physical heart system.

But here is the bottom line. You may not care about metaphysics but you may want to do something about health and wealth.

Spend more time in the heart you say
It in charge is a better way
Ego is not the creator, make it clear
Stop giving life to energy of fear

HOLLOWPHYSICS | HOLOGRAPHIC

**What our science says today
Is mostly changed on a future day
If you believe only what you see
That vision will indeed limit thee**

What we see, read, hear, are told, and experience all goes to forming our beliefs. Where miracles are concerned, it appears to be the, read, hear, are told by science and medicine that we surrender our beliefs to, taking on what they say. So the experience doesn't happen. Seeing seems to be irrelevant. But have you ever considered that if you believe first, then the experience can happen? Then read, hear, told are irrelevant. This is how Seeing is Believing gets shifted to Believing is Seeing?

This chapter is for the logical left-brained, rational science followers who *will not let go of science*. You believe seeing is believing and if there is not a qualified scientific explanation then, you don't pay attention. Obviously the best scientists still seem to ignore what they see anyway. This chapter is about physics and metaphysics. It is short because it can't really contribute to helping you with healing miracles or co-creation. Where it can contribute, however, is to show you that physics, the kind that expounds on its "science" of matter is a huge joke with less credibility than miracles. Enter Quantum Physics. Here we rapidly see that the best Scientists on the planet don't have a clue as to how to correct the inadequate "Laws" of material physics.

Here is the conundrum: Newtonian material physics explains about 3% of the physics of matter and non-matter. It is based on laws that reflect solid matter, 97% of which is space (hollow), to explain things. So laws that explain 3% are deemed by assumption to explain the rest. Why? Because we are told so. Metaphysics on the other hand, which includes the 97% too, is explained by quantum physics as being holographic. Why the big conundrum? It seems that a totally unscientific force called consciousness seems to have something to do with that material 3%.

Why is this important here? Well, if you are clinging on to what science says about what I have said in the first chapters, think again. You have to drop the limits of the walls of belief in physics before you can let anything else into that mind. You have to let go of the limits because they are simply non-science anyway—better termed as nonsense.

To quote many new scientists who struggle with these issues:

"Experiments have demonstrated that the worldwide view implied by classical physics is wrong. Not just slightly incorrect in minor ways but fundamentally wrong in just the right way to support the reality of psi."

First of all, I was a scientifically driven scientist and businessman. Educated as a Mathematician, Geologist, and Computer Scientist, you could not get a more logic seeking Dude than me. My education put me into that particular box that formed my beliefs and hence habits, and hence my life. As my career led me to the upper echelon of the business world of power, profit, performance, and the bottom line, it got worse. It demanded a mind which was left brain pragmatic and logical, somewhat detached from the heart.

But those limits which at that time were perceived as career advantages, became somewhat restrictive to the other part of me—the Higher Mind. It was inevitable that a quest be initiated because of the dramatic ups and downs of this life. Some gut feel that there was more to my life than I was experiencing. It was inevitable that my family life shatter. That was the first paradigm shift. This was followed by my formal education on business and commerce being shattered. Then all of my geological and nature limits were shattered. The next shift occurred when my agnostic attitude became shattered, and then, lo and behold, my scientific world of physics was shattered. Needless to say, that was a lot of glass on the floor and those limiting windows left very little in my belief boxes that could be sustained. It all just evaporated out. But the grand part was that it could now be filled again.

The problem with science is that of using references. Anyone who has an idea, concept or pet belief can write a book on the topic and become an instant "expert". The way you do this is to use statistics to show what you want to show, or quote another "expert" that supports your own belief. We all do this because it is the rational process by which you gather supporting or collaborative information. The more you gather, the greater the evidence supporting your belief and the bigger the expert you are. Well, this is great in principle but in practice it is not the way to the truth because anybody can try to prove anything if they really set their minds to it.

Now there is nothing wrong in this because it does indeed help lead to new concepts, ideas and discoveries but it may also reflect bias and subjective motivations to a preferred theory or ego need. In many cases, to support an idea, it is necessary to go outside the laboratory and look at what is happening in the lab of life. However, the true value of science to me is that when science fails, the science of gathering information becomes crucial so as to support or discredit whatever the theory is. My science does not deny the existence of some phenomenon like miracles simply because they cannot be explained.

So here is the bottom line. If you hold on to left brain science limits with regards to miracles and co-creation, don't. They limit you. Zero out your mind on this. But, just in case, there is an issue here, I will direct you to some books which I will summarize. These particular books are filled with cases, examples, references, analysis and discussions on quantum physics and metaphysics.

Our entangled minds

The book that is mind shifting on this issue of psi; short for psychic phenomenon. The book is ***Entangled Minds Extrasensory Experiences in a Quantum Reality*** by ***Dean Radin[4].*** This book will save you a lot of inquiry time. Dean is a PhD (if that is important to you), and Laboratory Director at the Institute of Noetic Sciences in Petaluma, California. For several decades he has conducted research on psychic phenomenon at Princeton, the University of Edinburogh, the University of Nevada, and three silicon valley think-tanks as a scientist investigating the psi phenomenon.

This book will lead you through the psi world of telepathy, clairvoyance, psycho kinetics, remote viewing, dreaming, conscious-unconscious psi, mind matter interaction, gut feelings, presentment, global consciousness, reading the future, and many other

---

[4] http://www.deanradin.com/

metaphysical phenomenon. Dean shows how these are real, based on thousands of controlled lab tests. He surveys the origins of this research and explores the reality of our entangled minds, setting a new stage for a rational, scientific understanding of psychic experience. He debunks the skeptical myths.

The book is a unique adventure into debunking skeptical myths on the basis of controlled lab experiments and the reality of the new quantum physics. To quote Dean:

"There is a rising tension between the leading edge interpretation in physics and the tail end of metaphysics. Physicist interested in quantum ontology are painfully aware that some interpretations of quantum reality are uncomfortably close to mystical concepts. In the eyes of mainstream science, to express sympathy for mysticism destroys one's credibility as a scientist. Thus the taboo persists."

What is particularly important about his book is his treatment of quantum physics, explaining it, the conundrum surrounding it that has physicists in a bind, and how it explains our "new realities" of mind-matter. Once again, to quote Dean:

"Experiments have demonstrated that the worldwide view implied by classical physics is wrong. Not just slightly incorrect in minor ways but fundamentally wrong in just the right way to support the reality of psi."

Our holographic reality

The next book that is for the pragmatic logician is one by **Michael Talbot**, called **The Holographic Universe**[5]. This is a mind blowing treatment of the nature of our reality.

---

[5] http://www.crystalinks.com/holographic.html

Talbot describes the Universe as a giant hologram containing both matter and consciousness as a single field—a kind of image or construct created in part by the human mind. Using the world's most prominent scientists and thinkers, Michael weaves a mind-blowing revelation that there is room in science for the consciousness, the soul and spirit. Using the work of David Bohm one of the most respected quantum physicists, and Karl Pribram, the respected scientist on the human brain, he explains how the unsolved puzzles such as telepathy, out-of-body and near death experiences, lucid dreams and mystical experiences such as feeling of cosmic unity and miraculous healings are explainable through the holographic universe and quantum physics.

This treatment of the topic is filled with hundreds of cases and scientists that have gone against mainstream science to uncover the answers as to how holograms explain our world. The work of some of the best scientists on the planet points to our reality as holographic. The many cases and examples of science shattering are presented here and it is a must read, not only to understand how quantum physics does explain metaphysics, but how the holographic model of reality is the greatest revelation in science even though it is essentially ignored.

The reality of healing miracles

In this light, I bring to you my latest book ***Miracle, Miracle, I wish to Find Where you Hide Within My Mind***[6]. It has a purpose of studying the occurrences, experts and the practitioners of healing miracles. Yes they are not necessarily consistent and repeatable. But my quest is not to discredit, or to highlight that they are

---

[6] www.edrychkun.com

inconsistent, but why they are inconsistent, what is the common denominator when they do work, and what one can do to have one of their own.

The book focuses on well known cases, many filmed and documented in the books the authors have presented from their own experiences. In this book I cover miracles in history, religions, energy healers, native practices, near death experiences, placebos, faith healers, regression therapy, with God, without God, and solicit information from "the other side." I do not want to repeat this here but for anyone who does not think healing miracles are real, or that there is no benefit to considering them in their own health plan, this information will save you much time.

What has become loud and clear is that there really is no explanation of miracles and the so called metaphysical or psychic phenomenon. Regardless of how much you or science struggles with this, the answers are not in mainstream science. Thus, as I have alluded to many times here, you have to understand three things:

1. There is no mainstream scientific explanation
2. Miracles do occur and are real
3. Miracles can benefit you

Now do not get me wrong, science is great, it has created wondrous things, but it has created limitations as well. What I speak of here is the science and technology related to miracles and psychic phenomenon—metaphysics. It involves a huge list of esoteric abilities that people have that cannot be explained, rationalized, or replicated. So they get relegated to the nutcase and anomalous peg board of science.

Us vibrating humans

Valerie Hunt[7], a physical therapist and professor of Kinesiology at UCLA, developed a way to confirm and measure the human energy field. For example, Doctors use EEGs and EKGs to measure electrical activities of brain and heart for example. She discovered the EMG Electromyograph measures the energy field in muscles and expanded into the aura. Normal frequency range in the brain is 0-100cps (cycles per second) most occurring between 0-30cps. Muscle goes to 225cps, heart to 250 but this is where electrical function associated with biology drops off. She picked up a field of energy radiating from the body that ranged between 100 and 1600cps.

These were strongest in areas of the chakras. She noted the field behaves holographically as do the energy fields of the body and that these fields were non-local—could be measured anywhere on the body. She called it the holographic field reality. When the main focus of consciousness is on material the frequencies are in lower range around 250cps. People who have psychic abilities and can heal are 400-800cps. People who can go into a trance and channel other information operate in a narrow band of 800-900cps to receive information.

Those who are mystical are above 900—those who possess the wisdom to know what to do with the channeled info—aware of cosmic interrelatedness of all things and are in touch with every level of human experience. They are anchored in both psychic and trance abilities, but their frequencies extend beyond of up to 200,000-cps

---

[7] http://valerievhunt.com/ValerieVHunt.com/Valerie_Hunt_EdD.html

So is there a progression of psychic abilities? If you look at the A-Z of psychic abilities, there are some 200 listed. But the main ones are; After life communications, Aparitioning, Apportation, Astral projection, Card reading, Channeling, Clairvoyant, Déjà vu, Divining, Divine Intervention, Invisibility, Empathy, ESP, Levitation, Materialization, Necromacy, OBE, Ouji, Past Life Regression, Palmistry, Psychic healing, Remote Viewing, Regression, Scrying, Tarot, Tea Cup Reading, Telekinesis, Teleportation, Telepathy, Transfiguration.

What Valerie is saying is that there is a relationship between the vibrational frequency of the body's electromagnetic system and specific psychic abilities? Hmmmm... this is what we refer to as *raising one's vibration*!

Science is the observer of itself

At first thought, after delving into the conundrum called the "Observer Effect" in Quantum Energy, a silly notion came to me. First the Observer Effect says that the natural state of electrons is waves that have not formed into anything solid. The solid, or that which is perceived to be solid arranges itself into an atomic structure of electrons around a nucleus when consciousness observes it. Take the attention off and these electrons are back into their wave state. The notion was that the observation processes of experimentation and statistics actually creates the outcomes that it is expecting, so how can it go beyond? I understand that most scientific discoveries come from "way out" inspirations that no one knows where it came from. Then the other group is the one that expects nothing and has an open mind to let go of what they know.

That and the notion that this is all a hologram which our brain, a hologram itself is the filtering device that uses sense to make it take a different property in the hologram is pretty hard to conceive for even the highest IQ.

The chapter therefore is short. It is because science cannot answer the real question about how Faith, Love, Trust, Surrender work with regards to miracles. The answer does not come until you let go of the questions. What these books do, however, is empty your cup to the status of a child simply because you realize that not only do they not know the answers, they very appropriately confirm that what we know is totally inadequate, and at the same time they serve to underscore that these unexplainable miracles happen and are real. So the more you dig, the more you read, the more you realize you are digging in the wrong place looking for the wrong thing.

So in a sense it is useful but those who have broken through to know the answers and live them are those that let go and see much of this science as a quirk in reality.

At some point in your life, you created a solid wall that divides the two worlds of visible and invisible. All your experiences and perceptions created this. It is congealed into apparent solid bricks as a result, preventing you from letting go of what you have been programmed to accept as truth. This is the wall that divides the polarity, unity worlds of your life. When an NDE occurs, you float through this wall. When a miracle is performed it is from the other side of the wall. Whether you will walk through this wall in this lifetime depends on how you let go of the beliefs that created it.

Most of my writings are scientifically based. They try to explain these invisible forces and metaphysics through science. What I have learned is that science cannot explain these things and you have to look beyond. Science is wonderful in presenting facts of what does exist. These books I have presented bring forward the best minds on the planet, attempting to study what exists. They also are wonderful presentations of thousands of cases that are real, have happened, and cannot be fully explained. Miracles and incredible psychic abilities exist. They cannot be discounted or relegated to weirdo clinic simply because they cannot be explained.

The chapter is for you to shorten your scientific quest if that is what you are on. Read the references. These will make you realize that the experts do not know and the experts are the ones doing the studying. So that tells me what I know is that I need to let go of what they say and look to my own way of finding answers. The brick wall is solid until you let go, open up, and float through.

**Why should I to this non-science cling
When it can't even explain no thing
It seems more prudent to empty my cup
Then let my heart fill it up**

HOLD ON | LET GO

When you finally let it all go
There is nothing you need to know
The Higher Mind its command will take
The heart knows not what is a mistake

So how do others let go?

We let go all the time. We take on others opinions and experiences all the time. We surrender to the idea that if someone else is perceived as smarter, more powerful, an expert, it is simple to surrender to that , place it in your mind, then translate that in daily energy to apply it in your life. But when it comes to emptying your brain on certain things, letting go so the heart and the Higher Divine Self take command of your life, that's a whole different matter. You say I don't quite get how or why.

A most dramatic case of using these words in the context of shifting into the other Higher Mind of the Divine partner is underscored by a well known spiritual writer, **Eckhart Tolle**. In his first book, the **Power of Now,** he sheds some light on letting go of the old mindset in a rather extreme case. Eckhart had many little demons that he held onto that screwed up his life. In his book he explains the ultimate despair that led him to fall into a fear void. He probably had the equivalent of a near death experience that re-birthed his life. At the depth of his depression, the soul seemed to take over and he *let go* of everything that his dismal self had clung onto. He sat on park benches for two years in a state of joy and then became a spiritual teacher. His story as taken from his book:

"*Until my 30th year I lived in a state of almost continuous anxiety interspersed with periods of suicidal depression. One night after my 29th birthday I woke in a feeling of absolute dread... Everything felt so alien, so hostile and utterly meaningless that it created a deep loathing of the world. The most loathsome thing of all was my existence. What was the point of the misery? I could feel the deep feeling of annihilation, for nonexistence, was now stronger than the instinctive desire to keep living.*"

"*I repeated over and over that I cannot live with myself any longer. I suddenly became aware that there was two of me: the I and the self that I cannot live with. Maybe only one of us is real. I was so stunned that my mind stopped. I was fully conscious but there were no more thoughts. Then I felt drawn into a vortex of energy, slow then accelerating. I was gripped by fear and started to shake. I then heard the words resist nothing spoken as if in my chest. I felt I was being sucked into a void within myself rather than outside. Suddenly there was no fear and I let myself fall into that void. I had no recollection after that.*"

"*When I was awakened by a chirping bird outside my window, I had never heard such a sound before. My eyes were still closed and I saw the image of a precious diamond. Yes, if a diamond could make a sound that is what it would sound like. I opened my eyes. The first light of dawn was filtering through the curtains. Without any thought, I felt, I knew that there is infinitely more to light than we realize. That soft luminosity filtering though the curtains was love itself. Tears came into my eyes. I got up and walked around the room. I recognized the room and yet I knew I had never truly seen it before. Everything was fresh and pristine as if it had just come into existence. I picked up things, a pencil, an empty bottle, marveling at the beauty and aliveness of it all.*"

"That day I walked around the city in amazement at the miracle of life on earth, as if I had just been born into this world. For the next five months I lived in a state of uninterrupted deep peace and bliss. I could still function in the world although I realized that nothing I ever did could possibly add anything to what I already had."

"It wasn't until several years later after I had read spiritual texts and spent time with spiritual teachers that I realized what everybody was looking for had already happened to me. The intense pressure of suffering must have forced my consciousness to withdraw from its identification with the unhappy and deeply fearful self, which is ultimately a fiction of the mind. This withdrawal must have been so complete that this false, suffering self immediately collapsed. What was left was my true nature as the ever-present I Am: consciousness in its pure state prior to identification with form."

"I learned to go into that inner timelessness and deathless realm that I had originally perceived as a void and remain fully conscious. I dwelt in states of such indescribable bliss and sacredness that even the original experience pales in comparison. A time came when I for a while had no relationship, no job, no home, no socially defined identity. I spent almost two years sitting on a park bench in a state of the most intense joy."

"Later people would ask if they could have that which I have. I would say: You have it already. You just can't feel it because your mind is making too much noise. That answer grew to be this book."

"Unless you learn to recognize the false as false—as not you—there can be no lasting transformation, and you would always end up being drawn back into illusion and into some form of pain. Don't read with the mind only. Learn to watch for a feeling-response as you read and a sense of recognition from deep within. It is a reminder of what you have forgotten. Something within you will say, yes I know this to be true."

The main pitch is that you need to let go of your usual Lower Mind—ego—that runs your show. Here we see what happens when things really go awry and that Lower Mind takes control. While you look for material things and scraps of fulfillment, you have within you the great treasure. It is incessant mental noise that prevents stillness of what he calls *being* and casts a shadow of fear preventing enlightenment. His thesis is that you normally don't use your mind, it uses you. You believe you are your mind. You cannot stop thinking so you are not in control and enslaved. When you let go of this and truly recognize it as enslavement, you can then let your Higher Divine Mind—your other self take over.

Dramatic? There are millions of cases like this. Near Death and Out of Body Experiences are rife with vivid and dramatic examples. It's the same paradigm shift. The main point here is that the mind creates a brick wall called belief between the two worlds—the one where you hold onto the old self; where the laws of attraction/manifestation prevail, and the other, where you let go and let the laws of co-creation and materialization prevail.

So does one need to engage in such drama to trigger the change? Some people can quit smoking cold turkey. Others may take a few months of perseverance and some can't do it. We are all different of course, but what is the real difference here. Obviously willpower, is it not? It depends on how strongly encoded into your belief system—and hence your cellular memory—as to how much you really need that smoke. The bottom line is that eventually you have to convince yourself and no matter how much science or statistics or others frowning at your nasty habit bug you, it is mostly irrelevant until something convinces you to take action, change your belief and create a belief you can do it.

There are millions of cases of people letting go, surrendering to something greater—even if it is a placebo, a hypnotist, energy healer, or God. Some had to die, or have something dramatic like a NDE or OBE where they came back and things were just a wee bit different.

At the other end of the Tolle spectrum are the miracle healers that I studied in my last book. They did not let go completely like him, they learned to let go for a short time only even if they were not aware of it. Many are not aware of it but what they are consistent on is that they are surrendering their powers to a higher one and trusting "it will be done". How did they do that?

Well, here is another bottom line about healing miracles. When you know that you don't really know, nor care how miracles work or are explained, and it really doesn't matter, then that is letting go. What you feel in your heart is that it simply works (Faith). It is your heart (Divine) that will take care of it (Trust). There is no need to be intimidated, have doubt, or be conscious of past or future; and there is no need to keep awareness on how it is done (Surrender). It is this instant that is important (Now). You are not sure how you will even know (no Expectation or Conditions) what will happen and you will simply try to feel changes or instant guiding. You have no conditions (Unconditional) on it and are entering a Divine partnership (Co-creator).

It's like saying: *"Hey Dear Divine Partner in the heart, I am here with you visiting. I love you and here is that issue that is now gone so there is a void for you to make perfect again. Let me know when you are done, thank you."*

Will it work for you? I don't know. It could. Perhaps you are not the cold-turkey-quit-smoking type. Maybe you need to practice it. Just never let go of the thoughts that it will work for you. How long do you have to try? Until it works. When do you know it works? When it does.

There is a transition I have found but it is pretty hard to do the whole thing cold turkey when you have to work for a living and depend on a pay check. But those are the ties that bind. And it isn't until you realize the Laws of Attraction and Manifestation that the chains suddenly loosen.

What I had to get used to was that if something met with resistance, then it was not the path to follow. If something went wrong, it was meant to create a marker sign in the road to teach me something right. If something did not happen, it was because it was not meant to. Something else would come along as long as I did not fill my mind, and attention with what went wrong or what I had to do to make it happen. That is called following the path of least resistance and coincidentally, it seems to turn out to be a passion. It is like a set of prods that poke you when the wrong path is taken. The body does the same. It is a gut feel or an intuitive thing that says: *"No, we don't think so Dear One, it just is not right for you."*

But the toughest one of all was my soul friend from many, many lifetimes back would say: *"If you want to make God laugh, tell him your plans."* Your plans are indeed written and that is to use free will and the Divine to have the best life possible, regardless of what it is that you contracted to do, and regardless of what type of energy confronts you. It is called passion and bliss and anything else is shorting you and your life.

I was trained to be a scientist. I graduated in Mathematics and Geology. I was taught what the best minds knew. I went into business, computer research, marketing, banking, economics and top executive positions to create and run companies. I learned what all the best minds said worked best. But it never got the answers that I was seeking. Who am I, what am I, what am I here for, and why can't I have a wondrous life off the gopher wheel of commerce.

The answer was not in science. It was in non-science. All my writings had been into that scientific jungle of conflicts, opinions, egos, and conflicting statistics. Most people I understand have about a 3 minute tolerance for science. For every opinion stated by an expert, there is another opinion that contradicts it. So how important is it? It is not. You end up believing what you believe because someone else convinces you and because it has the strongest morphic marketing field. Did you check with your heart? Intuition? Gut feel? In line with passion? No, not really. It is not "scientific". It is not logical. It is not rational. Ya da ya da ya da.

So here is my first book on the topic that is not going to spew scientific stuff simply because the words love, consciousness, quantum, energy, faith, trust, and let go are scientifically illogical, unquantifiabe, undefinable, just like words gravity and magnetism. Can you imagine how long it would take a scientist to simulate with formulae the frying of an egg or explain what gravity really is?

I like to ask those planetary scientists a simple question: If I dug a hole from my yard, standing up, all the way through the middle of the Earth, how would I come out on the other side—head first or feet first? Would I emerge like through a ceiling or would I fall out? Think about it. You can get a room full of scientist to argue about this all day. Why? It's a simple question, is it not? Maybe things are not as we think they are?

So if you are still a pragmatic, logic seeking, doubt-filled left brain human that will not believe anything that you do not see, or are not able to form your own truth, then there are certain recommendations for you in the chapter you read called **Hollowphysic|Holographic**.

But I caution you. They do not, and cannot answer the real question about how Faith, Love, Trust, and Surrender work with regards to miracles. The answer does not come until you let go of the questions and determine your own meanings—and believe it. What these books on physics do now, however, is to empty your cup to the status of a child simply because you realize that not only do they not know the answers, they very appropriately confirm that what we know is totally inadequate, and at the same time they serve to underscore that these unexplainable miracles happen and are real. So the more you dig, the more you read, the more you realize you are digging in the wrong place looking for the wrong thing.

So in a sense it is useful but those who have broken through to know the answers and live them are those that let go and see science as a quirk in reality. Do you know how you would come out on the other side of the planet? It is round isn't it?

What is it to Let Go?

It was in late 2009 as I approached the end of that book that I began to understand what letting go meant. It was when I began to communicate with my Divine Self and the "other side" that it became clearer. First I found out that there is a sharp dividing line between manifesting and co-creation. It is because all energy is in one of two states. If you are attracting and manifesting then you are dealing with bringing energies to you resulting in experiences that you desire. These *already exist* as situations, people, things, and so on. But if you are Co-creating energies, you *create* things you desire. These may be completely new energies that form into matter instantly—like miracles.

There is a progression here. The two main states of energy are some-thing—an atomic material state, and no thing—a wave state. The progression goes from attraction to manifestation to Co-creation to materialization to Creation. I want to repeat this because it is important. With the Law of Attraction, it means creating the energy that attracts like energy waiting for it to bring you the experience.

Then there is the Law of Manifestation. Once you figured out the attraction and understand you are attracting like energy, now you start realizing that you are like a magnet pulling events and things to you. But this is also from matter that is already created. From these people, things, and situations comes your personal perception of the experience. From the sea of quantum energy that sits around waiting for consciousness to do something, your choice becomes one of simply letting this happen without awareness of its process, or being aware of the energy process and managing it to your needs.

If this is working on "autopilot", typically it is the Lower Mind, your ego and the part of the mind focused on your material needs, instincts, and comforts that prevail in creating the energies. That is the attraction-manifestation side which you may or may not be aware of.

But there is the Higher Mind where the Law of Co-creation unfolds—like when a miracle suddenly materializes, and then you start the journey to the Law of Materialization, when you can create anything instantly. The Higher Mind is where all thinking and action is "heart-based". It is the realm of love and compassion, of reverence and peace. It is higher vibration energy. This is where the "co" comes in—the heart, the Divine, the partnership that allows new energies to be created from no thing.

That is the big dividing line on the cover, centered on the Heart. It is a solid brick belief wall that can be knocked down by letting go of the laws of classical physics and many other things that create doubt in your mind. So on one hand, you are attracting energy of desire from the existing atomic world of "solid particles"—your usual Lower Mind. On the other hand, when you get into the Higher Mind you are creating something into the atomic state from the quantum state where only waves and no thing exists. It is an evolution. Why do you need to let go? It's because the partner of yours—the Divine Co-creator Higher Mind lives in this quantum space where no thing or nothing exists. So to get its help, you have got to follow few rules.

When you leave the old lower mind of memories behind and attain the partnership with the other higher mind you receive inspirations because you do not have to think anymore—that higher mind thinks for you. Changing to this state of mind is related to how you think. In reality there is nothing new here because most of the time your ego and lower mind are already doing the thinking for you.

These rules are clear on this division. Either you partner with your Divine Higher Self or you don't—there is no try as Yoda said. The partnership has a code of behaivor and when you understand these simple words and enfold— yes enfold these the way they were meant to, miraculous things happen. In their raw simplicity these are very powerful words as they can guide the architecture of your life and reality. But they can also be dysfunctional energies that have no clear purpose if they are not deployed in accordance with Divine Law. We will get to this eventually but the bottom line is *what do they mean to you* AND are the actions resulting from them *relecting genuine beliefs?* It has to do with YOUR individual perception and understanding of those words. What do they mean to you?

How do I let go of what I know?
I spent a lifetime making it so
You did indeed said the heart to me
Place it on the shelf and let it be

OUTSIDE | INSIDE

Who is it that speaks to me?
It is not from one that I can see
Must I first go out of my mind?
To seek the answer I want to find

I have learned to let go of what I know each morning before the usual outside hum drum of life captures me. I am getting better and better because my belief system supports the need for the paradigm shift towards the inside where my Divine Partner dwells. During this period, I essentially zero out what I know from my outside—my everyday world—to listen to and communicate with the inside—my heart and my Divine Partner. At a point in the quest for miracles, I realized I could do this by intending to and realizing that when I zeroed out, most of the thoughts that bubble forward are not really mine.

First, I had to deal with my terrestrial ego buddy that has all these issues of yesterday and tomorrow and all those usual things that you end up dealing with during the day. What happens when I get rid of that and move into a quiet space—I get new thoughts and a download of information (sort of like channeling) that now happens like a telepathic conversation.

In this case, I address the Ascended Master Sananda, but at this level we are all One communicating telepathically. As bizarre as this may seem, the information is telepathic from within me and through me. It is a process whereby Sananda activates it. The process has brought forward some very profound messages that ended up not only reinforcing much of what I had learned, but adding answers that were new. This is all documented in my latest book, ***Miracle, Miracle, I Wish to Find Where You Hide Within my Mind***[8], where I tell the story of how this happened and bring forth some of those revelations. Of particular interest is the information given me on Manifesting and Miracles. I want to summarize this here because it helps to understand how we must first ground our beliefs on the left (Polarity) on the outside of the process. This is what we begin to understand how to let go of and move into the right side of Unity on the inside. What follows are selected sessions that were directed at me to explain this.

The process of Co-creation

"We note that the area of manifesting troubles you as you are constantly trying to analyze it. We think that you need to let go of that and simply begin to accept there is doubt in analyzing. We prefer to refer to this process as Co-creation because it is more relevant to what actually happens in manifesting. You are a Co-creator of your life and you do have the ability to materialize or co-create at a new level. You have a Divine Partner in this process and although you are already doing this automatically, you have not quite got the process unobstructed by your intellect. Yes, you are co-creating all the time because you do not even think about it."

"It is automatic and your belief and intent of this is synchronized because you have no obstacles in believing that negative things can come your way—it is the way of it, right? Do you think you will attract negative energies

---

[8] www.edrychkun.com

in your life by creating anger and conflict? After all, you have had many lifetimes, and many years of practice in embedding this in your beliefs. Your memories are full of these thoughts. But positive things come the same way. You do not even knowingly attach yourself to the outcomes because you believe there is no connection. Of course you don't want issues and problems, but by placing your thoughts, images, words and feeling onto these issues and problems, you end up with more of the same. So you automatically generate these discordant energies at will, and ask for your co-creating partner—which is really your Higher Self—to help attract and manifest them. So you are very practiced at creating the energy, giving it life, disconnecting yourself from an outcome, and waiting for the experience—even though you don't want it—ironic isn't it? Yes, you are adept at autopilot reactive attraction and manifesting already."

"But when it comes to proactive co-creation, it is an entirely different matter because you may have a shadow of doubt, or be insecure as to the process, be too attached to the outcome and dilute the energy of desire so it sits there in a transition state. Yes, we have told you before that you create energy instantly and it waits for you to congeal or materialize it by your actions and intent. Of course the power of this energy is related to how you align your thoughts, visions, words and feelings. And of course others, and crystals, can help to amplify this as well. This is where reinforcement of that energy clarifies the outcome and further energizes it into being. But if there is doubt within you, and your beliefs are not aligned, then this serves to delay, dilute or even dissolve the power of a result. These are the limits and blocks that you impose on the process. And for true proactive co-creation, where you are in control, you need to be very aware of your Divine relationship with your heart and eliminate your shadows of doubt."

"Let us back up a minute and note that your world which appears solid is simply in a different energy state and it has been created by the Creator consciousness. Everything in it which is simply a hologram of energy in a different dimension has life with a purpose of evolving. You as a physical body are integrated into this scene to play out your roles as you see fit to expand it and yourself. Within the movie you are able to co-create different ways. You can create, rearrange, or attract your creations and hence experiences. To create means to materialize something into a solid form. Humanity has a long way to go to do this but it is indeed possible to materialize something solid in front of you."

"You have come to know this in miracles—like those of healing. This is a process where after attention to a solution, and a Divine partnership is made in the heart, you detach from the outcome and rely on faith to prevail. And so as you understand it, the quantum state of waves, manifests itself into a new state of perfection— which is all we know—and it becomes a solid representation of what was sought as the desire. Eventually you will learn that materializing a solid object relies on the same process as you are simply adding to the hologram in your dimension."

"To rearrange is a similar process. It is one of changing the arrangement of the form into a new form that is solid. This is a transformation process as done in Alchemy which abides by specific natural laws. The partnership with the Divine, if not there, with the strong belief, is vital. Without it, nothing will happen."

"In the case of attraction, you are creating the energy that has specific vibratory qualities and strength attached by you. You do it daily. What occurs here is that this energy sits in a temporary holding area looking for other energies that will be attracted to it like a magnet. Here you are not creating the object; you are

attracting the objects, events, people or situations that already exist to provide you with the experience."

"Think about this like the little dots that you see on the movie screen of TV or your computer screen. They are simply dots configured into unique patterns that are meaningful to you and give you an experience. Yet they are not solid things in the screen. They are just little dots of energy composited into some meaningful expression of energy. The energies you create are similar. All you have to add is that these patterns on your screen are magnetic and they set up fields—which you call morphic—that eventually attract similar patterns. The time to do this depends upon the strength and your belief that it can be so. As we have pointed out, you are already doing this without thinking—and therein lies the big clue—you are not thinking about it. And without even knowing, you have let go of limits and are co-creating with your Divine counterpart. And yes, it can be negative or positive. The heart only knows perfection and it knows what is happening. And if it is not perfection, there will be a reaction in your body and Soul. You will feel this as dis-ease or disease or dysfunction—perhaps a feeling of discord."

The two pathways

"There are two paths related to this awareness. There is the Ego and the Heart. They are of course commanded through the mind which can determine which path you use. Both Ego and Heart can control or command your chemistry either automatically or by you, depending on your awareness. The Ego pathway into the manifesting field is what humanity usually relies on and your energy packets reach into the Divine—you call it Zero Point Field. They are simply commands to manifest as we have discussed. There is no distinction of bad or good, negative or positive, it is simply energy looking for a likeness—a mate. The Heart, on the other hand, knows

what is not perfection—that which is not love—and you will sense a discomfort when discordant energies are placed into the inventory."

"You may have many energies that are there waiting for you to enforce them by emotion, attention and alignment. They could even be from previous lives. If these energies of intent are weak or confused, they will sit there. If many of these weak ones are there, you can be easily drawn into other energy fields that are stronger and that is the way of it even if it has no distinct purpose. You then become a victim of other energies that have created their own fields which you call morphic. What this means is that you are letting your life be commanded by default, and if you allow your Ego to create the fear, attention and intent, then you are defaulting to what the Ego desires—not what your heart desires."

"When you by awareness of the Heart, and the Divine in it create the commanding partnership, then you can indeed change the nature of your manifestation in that they are more controlled and you become a true Co-creator. But the partnership relies on your belief and faith. Note that when it is on autopilot it is not even in your mind as it is not part of your doubting belief system. The Heart and the Divine are perfection and they strive to bring back that perfection when that partnership is clear like by non attachment, clarity, trust, faith, believe, and love based. The stronger this is the faster it congeals from temporary to visible energy. This is the secret to materialization which humanity is a long, long way from."

"So the path you choose is of your free will and the success is dependent upon your awareness and belief system. We encourage you to build this faith and relationship—to balance the Ego as its decisions if left unchecked will affect your health, quality and length of

life. The body was designed to live long within the realm of the Heart. The control has been given to the Ego, to power, to gratification of the senses, to conflict over material things. These all have consequences to your body as a result. Shifting to the command center of the Heart unfolds a grand partnership as a true co-creator on a grand scale that you have yet to understand."

Let us expand on your Law of Attraction

"Yes, let us continue on manifesting, or co-creation. The one we want to talk about today is what you call the Law of Attraction. Think about how you create your desires—you want to find a new friend, or find something and you think about it, dream about it, feel it in your heart. You are creating waves of energy that create a field—you call it morphic—and it permeates other energies. It is like a swirling vortex of energy which builds a stronger charge depending on how much clear energy of desire you create. How does it do this? It is not difficult for wave energy because everything is connected as one—just like your DNA and you are part of the One—remember? So it is like matching particles that are magnetized. These permeate all that is One."

"Think again about your TV set and the particles that form images. Think about how these particles that give you emotions are nothing but specs of light, color and intensity that your senses interpret. These dots or pixels could have a magnetic pull that either individually, or combined, created a specific pull signature that looks for like energies and attracts them. Do these dots sometimes draw you? Yes, a hologram that can draw others! This is not a difficult concept except that it is not supported by your scientific wisdom."

"We shall continue on manifesting, in particular, this Law of Attraction that has captured so many. It is partly true but like many things on your planet, they are not the

whole truth and quickly gravitate to motivations of money and selling to those that are desperate or seeking wealth."

"We told you there are several pathways to manifesting. The Divine path is fast, while the manifesting path of attraction is not so fast. The attraction path manifests experiences where it draws to you the energies that have likeness. It draws to you the energies that you generate through your thoughts, visions, words and emotions. We have already discussed how the clarity of the desire, the alignment of these subtle energies dictates how rapidly the energy that you create draws or propels you to the like experience. This process is not creation, or co-creation, it is simply manifesting the experience of something desired by drawing the people, situations, things that already exist."

"Think about how you may do this in two ways that you are used to. First, you may want to create something, or do something to have an experience—say it is flying or climbing a mountain. You simply plan it and away you go to have it. Sometimes it may be more complex, so you create a business plan and follow the activities you have outlined to make this experience occur. It may result in the creation of something as a result—like a business. You are used to this. It is all done in the outside."

"But then there is also another way and that is to create the energy of alignment and watch how you draw others into your energy field. You may want a house, or new TV, or new opportunity; then suddenly it is there as a choice for you. This does not mean the TV suddenly materializes in your house, it means that the TV may be seen at a store or it appears somewhere for you to make a choice on. Certainly you have to buy it and you may not have the money—so manifest the money as well. Clarity and alignment are vital. Remember this as this is an easier way, as you are letting the law of attraction

work for you after you clearly define what it is that is your desire and continue to energize it by reinforcement. It is done from the inside."

"Sometimes, you may be drawn into others energies as well. This is the way of it as you may have a need to sell something and someone else has a need to buy something. All that happens is that the two needs attract each other. How? Well, your energies penetrate everything depending on the strength and because all that exists is within you all, it is a matter of matching the energy signatures and drawing them like those little TV dots. This may be a local morphic field or a larger one. It may come from anywhere—an ad, a TV show, another person, but it is this drawing within the fabric of all matter."

"Now you are doing these two ways automatically all the time. That is how you create your world whether you know it or not. This way is not particular to the need or the type of energy you create. It is simply energy the laws respond to, negative or positive. Most are used to such strong alignments when it comes to fear that permeates your thoughts, visions, words and emotions. Most of you are good at this already. Clarity and focus are the key and continued attention reinforces the energy to make it resonate stronger."

"It is like a musical note. It has a specific tone or vibration when played. From 7 notes, you can create a song. These 7 notes can be combined into new patterns that are each unique. These can be played by different instruments making different tones and this can be combined into a magical concerto. These are all energy signatures looking to attract others of like sound. You are the orchestra playing the music. Your chakras are the original 7 notes and they can create any concerto you want if you use them. What are their musical

sections? Thoughts, Images, Words, Emotions, Intent, Relationship, Material."

"But now let us look at a much faster way of doing these manifestations and attraction. It is the Divine Path through the Heart. But we do not pay much attention unless it is aligned with the Heart—the Divine. So you can go ahead and manifest things bad or good and only feel the discord and ill feeling of the Heart if they are not aligned. But no one will stop this process. However, if you want to co-create—to change the very fabric of the material—like in a miracle that creates something like a new possibility in your mind instantly, you need to have a co-creator. That is us—actually you too. It is your Higher Self living in your Heart. And how do you get our attention?"

"Well, dear One, it is through knowing who you are and that you can indeed do this. That must be your belief. So yes, you need to have attention and thoughts and words and emotion but those are aligned for the higher good of yourself and all that is. Otherwise why would your Divine counterpart—your co-creator care to respond? But this does not require continued reinforcement—a healing miracle is instant—because it simply happens as a new possibility that takes you or something to its zero state of perfection. But it is the belief that limits—the belief of who you are and what you can do. So you need not drive yourself to distraction by affirmations. Simply place attention, go to your Heart, keep faith and trust that it will be. Yes, we know this is not easy but it is that simple. You have been doing some of this the hard way because you have not believed in your partner—your Co-creator that is part of you. And your Co-creator is Love—your Heart—it is you; that part which needs your 3D attention and belief to shift."

"So Dear One, this is the true way to change, co-create and manifest your heart's desires. You will see that this

will become easier and easier as the next year unfolds for you."

In simple terms there are four steps

"Yes, we continue as you still have questions about the process. Perhaps because you name this all as manifestation which is only one part of it. Let us look at this process as four steps. These are Attraction, Manifestation, Co-creation and Materialization. It is a progression from outside to inside, from unknowing to knowing or unconscious to conscious command. The first two have the Heart involved while the last two have the Heart engaged. The first two are your first major pathway we have discussed where you create any kind of energy in a holding area like an escrow and then passively or actively enforce the strength of it to attract and manifest an experience. The last two are active engagement in the partnership of the Divine—the Heart—to co-create an event, situation, or material object. While one simply attracts and manifests with existing matter, the other through the help of the Divine rearranges matter into something new."

"*Of course you know this second path as miracles. And you know that the Co-creator is your Higher Self which is part of the Divine. And you know that the key here is Belief, Compassion, Love, Faith, Trust and Gratitude, don't you? This does not require continued repetition like an assertion to manifest experience, only a strength of belief, a heart's desire to be perfection, a trust in yourself, a detachment from the outcome, a faith that it is so, and gratitude that it is done. Does it sound difficult for you? Yes, it has been difficult because you have not known yourself and you limit this through your belief by listening to other people who do not believe. And you are so busy analyzing it you cannot detach yourself to surrender and listen."*

"Yes, that is the way of it. So while your mind slumbers about this, you begin by your Law of Attraction and create a resonating field which attracts like energy. Then you may begin to realize that by managing your energies of thoughts, images, words and emotion, you can more actively manifest the experience. That you can call the Law of Manifestation because you are proactive."

"When you pass through into the next level and realize you are a creator and can rearrange matter and energy, you begin to co-create miracles by entanglement and collapsing of the wave forms into a new outcome. This is the Law of Co-creation. As you become stronger and your belief is undeniable, you then begin to create things by actually materializing them from the wave forms of energy. That is the Law of Materialization."

"Yes, prayer, meditation and connection to your Higher Self are your ways to develop this heightened awareness because they are high vibration actions of intent. It is through understanding your Higher Self partner is you, your heart, Divinity and such communication is the gateway to your subconscious Zero Point field of infinite possibilities."

"So who are you Dear One? Do you believe it? How clear and charged are your desires? And how rapidly do you believe your desires and materialize?"

And now miracles and emotion

"You ask us about miracles. Let us tell you more about something that is missing in your work. It is about the emotional body that envelopes you and in particular your heart. Your heart has many fields of energy that you are not aware of but the one we wish to speak of is the one that is referred to as the emotional body or feeling body. It is like a light bulb and is the most beautiful creation when it is lighted. Each of you has one and it is a radiant

light which emanates its colors and vibrations of excitement. The height and brightness is caused by the emotion from your heart—which is an energy of emotion generated from your sensory systems of taste, sight, smell, touch, and hearing. Think about the feelings that your body creates for you when you eat something wonderful, or see something beautiful, or touch someone you love, or smell a pleasing flower, or hear peaceful music. These are all incredible feelings that impact your emotional body and permeate your being in a harmonizing result."

"There is of course a hierarchy of these; unconditional love being the strongest. Compassion, bliss, joy, laughter, harmony, peace, gratitude are others that are very strong energies and make your emotional body pulsate with wondrous colors and brightness. Of course there are the opposites of fear and conflict that do not create the light and the emotional body dims and closes to the discord. This state in your emotional body is very important in your manifestations."

"For example, in your attractions and manifestations, the emotional strength is what gives the manifesting energy that you create with thoughts, visions and words its true power. The stronger this is and the clearer it is, the faster is the change from etheric energy created instantly to external energy that you can experience. The field which you refer to as a morphic field vibrates with excitement as it entrains with the emotional body. And as we have said, it matters not whether it is negative or positive because it is still energy you create. But if the energy is strongly negative, you can be drawn to other like energy whereas if it is positive, you will draw it to yourself. You must know that although your emotional body may be dimmer due to the discord and negative emotion, it is still energy and still has power to attract, but not with any divine co-creative partnership."

"However, Dear One, if you are to be a Co-creator, your partner does not hear you if you are not of a strong positive and pure emotional vibration. Its domain is perfection and it cannot be of assistance unless you are pure of heart and with a highly charged emotional body. You have learned that the Intent is first, the Pathway is meditation, awareness and prayer, and the means are the positive emotions or feelings created. These positive ones we mentioned are higher level energies of completion. You know that when the energies of thought, vision, words and emotion are aligned with the Heart's desire, and continuously enforced, you have the true secret of creating your own manifestations. Your strength and consistency in the emotional body will impact the speed at which the etheric energy attracts the physical energies. This is because the field excites the electrons that are the basis to all things and gets them to seek each other—they are all one anyway, remember?"

"But with miracles, or co-creation, be clear that the electrons common to both the etheric and material states become highly excited when the emotional body is positively charged with unconditional love and compassion. When this occurs, they are easily influenced to rearrange from a quantum perspective into a new possibility simply by changing paths, state and orbits into a different outcome or different atomic state which you sense and perceive as solid. And it is also here that we and the Divine Heart has its power to influence that new arrangement. But we caution you in that the emotional body cannot be fooled. Emotion is a universal energy and laughter can be false, or love can be with condition, or talk can be a lie. This does not fool the Heart and its emotional body. It is part of your belief system as well."

"Should you carry an ulterior negative motive in your laughter or your outward feelings that do not match your

internal Divine ones, you fall back to manifestation and attraction. Many may not even be aware of this discord and simply believe you are doing good. Sorry, that is not the way of Divine energy. It knows. It, like you for example pick up the discordant notes in a piece of music instantly even though the piece attempts to disguise it. Miracles occur when the emotional body of the Healer is strong, pure of heart and genuine—either directly by initial attention or indirectly through trusting the Heart. The most miraculous healers are of the purest state of high emotional body who enfold their patients."

"This is why you find that Healing modalities such as the Matrix Energetics that you have studied and practiced is so effective—but not with all. The lesson here is that one places the area of dis-ease on a peg board to create the focus and attention that it is gone. That picks up the vibration of it. Then by letting your mind go to the heart where you have a strong positive compassionate, unconditional loving emotional body, you disconnect yourself from the outcome by doing your 2-Point process of letting the Heart guide you to two different locations in the emotional body, connecting these, and trusting in the completion. This is Faith and letting go, or surrendering. Yes, it is indeed that simple but the purity and strength of the emotional body is not simple. The more you are filled with true and pure unconditional love, compassion, bliss, laughter and harmony the faster and stronger is the ability to facilitate the healing—or in this case rearrangement of the outcome. It is only in this space that your co-partner listens anyway."

"That outcome comes from the ability to co-create the excited electrons into a new form. And the degree of change depends upon the degree of light in your emotional body. In our next talk we will tell you about charging this emotional body of yours to a higher level."

Training the emotional body

"Yes, we will speak of the emotional body which you should institute in your 21 day Body Program (Note: See a later chapter on Rules | Covenants) *we spoke of. Part of this body program or code[9] you call it had to do with vitalizing your physical body with positive sustenance. In that code, there was a part which was to do with Silencing the Body which was to meditate quietly finding your place within which is in your heart. It is here that you should bring your favorite crystal to help amplify your energy. Simply place your crystal beside your heart and focus your attention on the beautiful emotional body that surrounds you. Ask the crystal to raise the vibration of the body, see blazing radiant colors and pulsating beautiful brightness around you centered on your heart. Give this five minutes of your time and try to see and feel the beauty and warmth of the love that radiates. See this field. Do this daily to become stronger, brighter and larger as it reaches outwards as far as you wish."*

"During your daily meditative session, you can practice the activation of your emotional body by reviewing wonderful experiences in your mind. Each of your senses can come into play as you simply place your attention on a wonderful taste, incredible music, enlightening words, majestic scenery, uplifting situations and experiences and so on that made your emotional body glow with excitement. Simply hold these wonderful experiences in your field of attention. Add your crystal if you want it to amplify the energy. Then you may do the same with the coming day's activities as you see the wonderful outcomes of the things that you plan to do. Look at each item and see a wonderful outcome resonate into your emotional body. A wonderful time to practice this is before you drop into sleep."

---

[9] Managing Human Subtle Energy: www.edrychkun.com

"During your daily activities, you must learn that you are there to change or convert discord to light. The first area of discord and disharmony will come from the papers you read, the news you hear, the problems you are surrounded with. Remember these are perceptions that convert to manifesting energy and that you are there to help change this, take a higher perception, or assist to make it better. Do not let these influence your emotional body. Your heart will tell you when these are not compatible."

"There are also the thoughts and visions that you yourself create by way of your ego or other matters that may come to you. Will yourself to not let these be of conflict, discourse and negative nature. Be careful to not give these any life and simply move to a higher place of perception with your Higher Self to change the energy to positive upon detection. Keep your emotional body protected from these by instantly acknowledging that they are not beneficial and eliminating or changing them."

"Then there are events and experiences that you may be drawn into or witness. These may be tragic, conflictive, or have a major impact upon your emotional body. These are to help you learn what you do not want or to show you how to move to a higher perception of good. Look to see something good that it created and place your attention on that."

"Then there are the plans and attractions and manifestations and miracles that you wish to create and co-create. These are as we have said earlier. Make a habit of creating these solutions and desires as completed, enjoyed so your emotional body totally engulfs the completion of it. Learn to solidify your belief, faith and trust in your Co-creator."

"As you follow this path, you begin to take command of your life and the true center of command begins to take over as the emotional body becomes stronger and brighter. It will completely change the experiences of your life as soon there cannot be any discord or limitations that can influence, penetrate or affect you. We suggest you do this as part of your 21 Day Body Code program and you will be very excited about what happens to your life."

Practice will change your beliefs

"So you want to create miracles. You already can and do but your confidence is still in doubt. Your beliefs limit you so we suggest you set up a special mantra that you can activate instantly when you are ready to do your healing. Let us do that now. Think of a special word that you will use as a mantra. Silence your mind and body then place yourself into your heart. Activate your heart crystal to see it glowing and ask it to amplify your heart's energy and the emotional body. Focus your attention on the beautiful emotional body that surrounds you. Ask the crystal to raise the vibration of the body, see blazing radiant colors and pulsating beautiful brightness around you centered on your heart."

*"Ask Archangel Michael to come to you and set the Sacred Fire Love ablaze in your heart and brain and your emotional body to purify and cleanse all discord and to replace it with the light and love of his Blue Flame. Ask me and Mother Mary to be present and assist in your healing and cleansing. List your will with your Higher Self. Feel the flame surge into the thoughts: **I will** myself to always be in my heart. **I will** myself to always react from the heart. **I will** my heart will always be ablaze with the Sacred Fire Love. **I will** my emotional body to always be bright and strong with a desire to live life to its fullest. As you feel this entering your heart and emotional body, then see healing energy coming out*

*through your hands into whatever you place them on. State your word three times **willing** it to represent that which you have placed your attention to. Then you state that this is your mantra and it will be activated by your simple action of stating it three times whenever you so choose."*

"Now, when you do your healing and drop into your heart, say your mantra three times and begin your session. We will help you and you will become stronger and stronger. When you do this to anyone, you will have them direct you to the area of dysfunction, place your hands in that area and visualize the healing energy projecting into it. By breathing and feeling the love energy vitalized and strengthened with each breath it keeps your energy flowing strong at a high vibration, drawing the low vibration dysfunction towards it. Low vibration cannot exists in a high energy of that from the heart and it dissolves it. Your client should be relaxed and of quiet mind. The energy will draw out the discordant one by raising the vibration to a place where it cannot exist. Ask Archangel Michael to replace old energies with new and to delete memories of it from all cells. Ask your client to see the area strong and perfect and ask them to feel the change as the energy cleanses. A suggestion of tingling or warmth will reinforce that a change is happening. You will know when this is complete."

"We would like you to practice your healing process as we talked about. You will find occasion to use it in the next weeks. Many have difficulty in staying on a spiritual path as they become immersed in their 3D material world. It is important to be grounded but we would like you to begin thinking about your divine desires instead of your earthly desires now."

"We also see that you are now used to moving into the heart, speaking with us and the angels. That is good and

it will be soon that you will be ready to travel to meet us in your wakened state. We will do this one day while you are meditating and see how it proceeds. You have asked the Sacred Fire Love to be with you and to enlighten your cells. Continue to ask Michael to boost that light into the cells as it will begin to connect with the Christ and eliminate aging. It will as you continue, work towards your bodies perfection. Be patient with it."

Remove limits stuck in your perceptions

"You are still very busy looking for analytical things like steps, reasons, processes and results. These logical left brain activities are interfering with what has no process or time. While you seek, you lose sight of the fundamental process of which there is none. It is a matter of releasing this and letting it be as it is in a natural way—it is this process that is your conundrum of limitation. You impose conditions, expectations, limits on how this works, steps where there are none."

"Let go of this and enfold the desire of being enjoyed, the emotion of joy fulfilled being part of the emotional body. It is what you must do to surround your need with feelings and emotion. That is it. Can you stop thinking, analyzing and inspecting things? Can you let go and really let others do the job? And trust that it is done? Can you thank someone before you see the job done? Can you love the outcome without any conditions attached?"

"Let go of steps and procedure. Surrender. Place attention on it yes, but then let go without expectation or signs of correctness. Look at these words that you analyze so much; attention, detach, surrender, belief, unconditional, faith, trust, gratitude, emotion. What do these words mean to you? Is your perception of these limiting you? Let us explain what they should mean:

Attention: *Can you bring the energy signature of something clear into your consciousness to make the mind aware of it? It is your attention that opens it for intention.*

Conditions: *Do you have any? These can create limits to the free energy. Do you think you have to be, do, or think a certain way for something to happen? Do not have conditions because there are none. Go to Zero—nothing—that is where your attention and intention are born into life.*

Faith: *How is this energy of belief living in your mind? Faith is Belief and Trust that you simply know—regardless of what anybody else tells you. Are there doubts that you are not deserving, it is beyond science, or you are not sure why? Keep the faith that you simply know it is so—no reason to expect, see, measure or feel otherwise.*

Surrender: *Can you let go of thoughts and knowledge and surrender to the higher power in the Divine Mind and Heart? To surrender is not to give in but to accept the existence and to detach from it. Suppose you had deformity at birth. Would you continue to place attention on it and feel the ills of it or would accept it is there and get on with what you can enjoy even though it is there.*

Detach: *Are you willing to detach your logic and knowledge of what is wrong or right, and let your Heart lead you? Can your mind be still like a child, enough to sense and feel what you must do?*

Emotion: *Is this feeling really being created? Is the completion of perfection in heart and the emotional body engulfed in the joy of it? Do you know it is the strongest ally when it is surrounded with emotion because that is the way you are designed. You create through attraction and emotion energies.*

Co-creation: *Do you truly understand your heart is your I AM essence, the Divine connection of you? Do you truly believe you, the I AM, is indeed that Divine power?*

Gratitude: *Are you able to know that perfection is done and that showing gratitude for its completion with the engulfing of joy or bliss signals completion?"*

"*Dear One, let go of logic and analysis of how this works. Do nothing except feel it and be led by it. Anything that does not do this sets up interference from the intellect and ego to confuse the heart field and block you from not becoming truly one with it.*"

"*Walk with your thoughts now and practice what you have learned. That is your main goal. It matters not how you define this except that you must have the faith to let go of preconceptions and relinquish control—like a child whose mind is an empty cup looking to be led by the parents. Practice this—empty your mind and become one with the heart as your parent. You will begin to blossom as the feelings of comfort and wonderful joy fill your being. You will know when you have suddenly transcended into this realm of miracles.*"

The information came from inside. It was telepathic because I gave the intention to create energy that needed answers. To me it began to explain things in a simple manner. What was happening was a paradigm shift from *believing is seeing* was changing from the old adage of *seeing is believing*. Intuitively I knew the truth was not in science so I did not look there anymore. I delved into the mysterious world of Polarity and non-science—that which the scientific community would prefer to call nonsense.

I am used to use my eyes
To see what around me lies
To visually see that for me
What seems to be reality
Behold I have a second eye
Not to scan what around me lies
But to create an image in my mind
So a new reality I can find

NOTHING | EVERYTHING

If inside is all that is
And knowing nothing is to know all
Then there's little for me to do
But live and love through and through

You may have heard the expression that when you know nothing, you know everything. What that refers to is simply letting go and temporarily forgetting all that you have experienced and learned. This is what meditation attempts to do when the Alpha or lower state is attained. It is a vibratory band where the busy conscious Lower Mind is effectively filtered out—like pouring sand over a fine mesh or tuning in to a specific band width on the radio. This space, as you drop down lower and lower through Delta and then Gama brings you closer and closer to the space at which that which is nothing vibrates.

It is where you are "inside" and "in the heart". It is where your attention, thoughts, memories, your intellect, everything can be "zeroed out". Yes, it is the Zero Field in quantum energy, the place where all is in vibrating wave state held together by a cosmic glue which we call nothing, or more appropriately no thing waiting for consciousness to make some thing. It is the sea of all possibilities waiting to be formed into some possibility—hence anything imaginable is already there waiting to be combined (collapsed) into an atomic state so a sensory system can experience it through the brain—your holographic filtering device.

It is typically not simple to do this simple thing of nothing but practice unfolds it as you learn to become present to your inside only. This, the opposite of prayer which *speaks* to this zero field of the Heart and the Cosmic Glue, is meditation where you *listen*. It is like being a curious child that knows nothing, always listening to learn new things that materialize as personal beliefs, behavior programs, and knowledge develops.

When you do listen, and tune into this space, because everything is interconnected, or as they say in quantum physics; entangled, it is where you have access to everything. Think about it like a new computer hooked into the internet. As you seek information, your favorite URL's become stacked with information portals that you seek, retrieve, and remember new information. What you have done, assuming you can, is let go of everything so you know nothing, handed over the control to the Divine and accessed everything. This is where inspiration originates but if you have no room because your current knowledge fills your disc space, then your beliefs prevent you from new information and change.

When you work with miracle workers and study what works, you get glimpses of how this state is attained. In retrospect, it is really no different than engaging in a conversation. If you are too busy trying to tell someone what you know as your opinion and your advice and belief will prevail so you are not really listening. It is less likely you will let any information in. You can "play stupid" and listen but then does it just flow through selecting parts that reinforce what you believe, or does it really replace the old with the new?

In further attempting to do this in practice, I raised many questions to the other side—my etheric consultants. The answers I received were once again not of this 3D world. They were from the other side of the veil. So I want to begin now with what they told me about this subject. It begins with a rather radical explanation of reality.

Parallel universes and holograms

"We begin our series but you must first know about parallel universes and holograms. As a Being of Light you use light to create your world which your body is a projection of. You use light to intersect beams of energy which in a primitive form is much like your hologram. Holograms are made of identical particles in different formations, the smallest component being reflected in the next size. If you should think about your pixels that are combined to create an image, sent to a receiver to display these, it is somewhat the same. A camera creates the image and the pixels are transformed and sent to a decoding system like your screens."

"Think about the progression of this, first a flat picture, then a 3D image which is just the way you fool your vision senses into believing it is 3D, then the next would be virtual reality where you and your senses are feeling like they are within it. The next stage is the hologram and then there is our reality which simply creates the hologram. Thoughts are like strings of pixels that work the same way as they are simply frequencies at a fundamental level of light intersecting and reacting to other energies."

"What is created is both fixed and static. That is a 3D world you live in as it is initially created is a living energy that grows, expands, evolves, and reproduces according to its instinct and encoded DNA—or chemical rules of Nature and the Cosmos. This like the earth and your environment are what we would call fixed. The interaction between them, through your consciousness,

and through your actions can change part of this which is static."

"That which is fixed is reasonably predictable as it abides by rules of love in the cosmos and nature but it still grows and expands and those beings that have free will, like you, can alter the static portion by will. You give life to other forms of energy and it grows, expands and flourishes, replicating itself. It is so with thought and the higher portion of you."

"And such a world is created by that Higher Self initially and statically modified by your will. A hologram is created and each part of the DNA is a reflection of the next largest to make the whole. Many such worlds are created or lived in by your light counterpart and it may choose its role, evolution and setting by projection—just like you project an image on a screen—like your cameras at a rudimentary level. They simply play out and use intent to will the static and fixed parts in the evolution, and in a timeless manner move between them."

Understanding the linear steps

"Let us begin with some linear steps that you humans are so preoccupied with. There is an evolution in this transition from sleeping to awakening to awakened to expanded, enlightened ascended. It is like the steps of attraction to manifesting to co-creation to creation or from 3D to 5D."

"It is where you learn to take responsibility, from engaging in what is created to taking full responsibility not only for what you create in terms of thoughts and feeling but in terms of the 3D reality in your life—the hologram."

"It is a transition like any solid form that in the Natural world of alchemy transmutes into a new form of energy

with differing characteristics. So ice sits and does nothing as it is low vibration. Add fire and it transforms to water which has more mobility and different characteristics. Continue and it becomes vapor, then it goes to no thing or nothing you call it but it is actually everything. It goes back to its state of perfection into the Zero Point quantum space of light particles waiting to coalesce into something by consciousness. It transforms itself into its spiritual energy of no thing."

"*We know you have trouble with this but it will come to you as you raise vibrations to new states and you reach that aah ha moment when suddenly it is all clear. How do you know? It just is. Is there doubt? No because you simply know. That is part of the evolution.*"

"*Suppose you were here and in another place. Now, in your 3D liner time, you have two worlds. You are here, then you go there. They are separate and can be completely different places. In your mind which is non-linear, you can go there instantly but you cannot yet window the two at the same time. This is right brain ability as it can multitask and respond to multiple programs or tasks at the same time. But you cannot yet take your body into both places at once. But from a time perspective, your mind can instantly transcend it. As you transist, you teleport or move into another dimension so your mind is already interdimensional. It is you and your left brain that is not. That is part of the transition.*"

"*Your Higher Self is already able to do this and does. It can create the holograms of different dimensions and it does not have a brain to limit it. Your brain is indeed a holographic filter or processor which is itself holographic. Your Higher Self is part of all of consciousness working much like your subconscious and your right brain multitasking high performance. The comparison is like the single thread slow processor versus the multithread image and symbol processor analogy that you are familiar with."*

"As you move from your linear step by step time to vertical stacked time, all of these lives and holograms are like a stacked pile of your DVD movies sitting on your shelf. You Higher Self can play these all at the same time in multiple windows and communicate telepathically all at the same moment because, like your right brain, it is designed this way."

"To you this is impossible because the left brain can only deal with one thing, one conversation, one movie, one situation at a time as it requires attention and focus in a linear progress. But when these are all playing simultaneously, every moment aligned there can be a multidimensional communication back and forth at the same instant like your multiprocessors."

"Your Higher Self is in the no thing world of love as the primary force. Feed it more and it transforms like the fire transformed the water. It has the ability to take the no thing and create some thing in the hologram."

"As you transist, this ability is rejuvenated in the properties you attain. This moves from being on the path of co-creation to actual creation and then becomes the Creator which is what you are in the first place. That is going Home so to speak."

"First you believe you are just you and you become involved with the people in your hologram, but as you begin to take responsibility for this, you understand that it is you that created it all. One leads to the other—it is as the method of Ho'oponopono says but it does not go the next step—at least it is not easily believed. So everything in your life created a perception, a behavior, thoughts, words, actions from all the things that come into your life. By taking responsibility for all this which is

in you, you can cleanse back to no thing that which is discord or dysfunction because it is your interpretation (no one else's) that creates that energy."

"But the more difficult truth is that you created all the players and the situations in the hologram—yes that is not a left brain concept. That is what the transition is all about. We are aware that this does not make sense but it will. It is important to remember that when you do take responsibility and take the power, there are some serious considerations as to how you use this power and that you must grow into with the wisdom of the Divine Creator that you surrender the ego to."

"In truth, once attained through higher vibration, if the power or fire of love (this is why we call it Sacred Fire Love belonging to Archangel Michael) is withdrawn and darkness comes back it is like the water turning to ice, and the properties are lost. So the will and the power of choice still rests with you. But as important change occurs in that the total interconnected nature of everything means that you begin to feel in you the discord of others, so if you attempt to hurt others it is the same as hurting yourself."

"The transition is one where the power is simply developed and actions move from control by the ego to command by the heart. Ego is designed to control survival, reproduction, growing, all encoded as instinct in their DNA. They all behave in specific ways to grow, survive, reproduce offspring and their social and protective habits support their particular biological or 3D structures. This is the way your outer self—your body— lives in this particular 3D world as well."

"The transition is to bring you out of this to higher abilities and merge with the Higher Divine Self. It means being lighter , higher vibration, and to ascend to awaken these properties and abilities to be able to multitask, be *multidimensional, to parallel process in the hologram that you create and to take the ultimate responsibility for what you create and created. What are these properties? They are the areas of miracles, psychic abilities, teleportation, levitation, apportation, telepathy, materialization and those area which your science deems as nonsense and your religions deem as heresy. Yet these are true powers you have given away to others."*

It is the letting go that takes you there

"Yes, this topic of letting go is heavy on your mind now and it is indeed part of the Great Transition. At night you have always automatically let go as you believe, and have the faith and trust that you will awaken in the morning and that your body will work, and the autonomic nervous system will do the right thing; and it does."

"When your senses in your body are felt in you as discomfort or pain you listen to these and respond to them, do you not? You temporarily listen and do what you think right or what the body is automatically programmed to do as its instruction for healing a pain or whatever is appropriate."

"But during the day can you let go of your world? No, you must do things, pay bills, go to work, fix the car, have a meeting. This is fine but are they driven by a passion or by the ego to survive. All of these habits and to do items are a result of your perception of past experiences and future anticipation of comfort and survival. These are driven by your perception as to why you must do these now—in the now. But there is a difference as ego is involved and as it is designed to be during wakening hours (just as spirit takes over at night unbeknown to you). Ego is driven by a need to use old experiences to ensure survival in the future, both as you know now are perceptions created by you."

"But what if you stopped this for a day? No plans, no to do's and let go of that? Can you do it? Can you listen to your Heart and simply be guided into the day and fill it with what you love, are passionate about, and produces bliss. You say it will not pay the bills. Yes and no. Can you do this for one day or two days? Try it… "

"You have learned that this is not instant and you must transist into the process of those four laws of Attraction, Manifesting, Co-creation and Materialization. Yes the dividing line is between them and it means Letting Go so that you have the faith that the bills will be paid and that you will be guided. Practice this and let go of your normal habits and things that you must do and substitute with things that are not planned and are simply the essence of your heart that desires passionately to do something."

"Do not let the ego interfere by saying but this, but that, or if I had this or that. Just do simple things at first that do not need huge sums of money—make these personal and simple at first. It is not an instant process as you have created habits over much time and many lives. It is a needed new practice as you have been programmed to not do this."

"Know the ego is past/future and the heart is now. Why heart, well you know this well. Think of the healing methods you know--Ho'oponopono and Matrix Energetics and others you have come to know. How do they let go and surrender to be guided? They give control to a higher power for a short time."

"Do it for a day and listen for joy and passion. Carry love and bliss with these activities. This is how the ego is balanced. Take the time of peace to drop into your heart and engulf the desire in emotion. You know all about this. It is your transition to finally letting go. It is when

you realize that there is indeed an easier way to pay those bills and you do not have to drum to egos tune and work all day at non-passionate things to do it."

"This is the transition to the four laws and the road to miracles. You have had ego on autopilot and it has had its way because it was designed to protect you and make those instinctual components of your DNA survive in your 3D hologram. Now learn to place your heart on autopilot and listen to it. The heart is Divine—Zero, yes where there is no thing and it awaits your design."

"You have noticed that your miracle workers have made the transition part of the time. They have surrendered to the higher power of their hearts and learned to listen. They have the faith they will be guided and sense and feel what they must do—which is essentially nothing. They zero out the mind, the intellect, the ego, and let go of it all for some brief moments. They have learned to listen a different way—what shows up, a change, an intuition, an action directed towards the higher good. It is where Divine inspiration lives instead of depending on memories which you hold onto that fill the mind. Can you do this not for a moment, but for good?"

The Process of Being

"Can you just be? It is a state in a void of nothing where no thing is there except everything waiting to be some thing. It is where you let go of your 3D world. A true state of being evolved back to what it is. You evolve and the transformation all your life and others as well so do not feel in a rush if this is not instant. It will occur in some instant where you are in your mystery of evolution through the different states of being. As you do evolve, say from instinctual to spiritual awareness you will have glimpses of the next evolution like miracles that you ponder over now. These are road signs of your journey."

"Otherwise, you expand, grow and enjoy. Then the big transition will occur when you let go. But as we have said you can let go slowly like one day, then two, then have a glimpse of what life can really be like and what these key words of belief, faith and trust, and surrender really mean. It is a transition from instinct to consciousness of all, to inspiration and to creation. At some point on your path your reality will let you know of the hologram you create from no thing and your whole reality will shift into the no thing or nothing because that is where the true power of love and everything really exists."

"There are many expressions surrounding the heart like I love you with all my heart, Heart of a lion, Heartfelt, Heart throb, Heartless, many. Where do they come from if the heart is simply an organ? You do not say I love you with all my liver, do you! It is because this is a high vibration energy field that the heart energy creates like a generator of heat. If a heat is generated and comes close when you are cold, your temperature will increase. If you are of the dark and you enter the heart, it will make you light, the same way. You must always stoke and feed the fire, must you not? But if you extinguish the love by constant darkness, how can it transist you? The heart, and being in it; in the sacred energy that It expresses, is indeed part of this critical transition into the place where you let go. Once in this field, this heart which is in the nothing field where Divine rules and all exists, is like a warm fluid that enfolds all that approaches it or enters it."

"It is peace, love, all of the wonderful properties but yet unformed into an experience of the solid hologram. As you transist from visible to invisible; from doing to being, you will change from relying on instinct, then memories, then go to inspiration, into the realm of No-Thing."

"At some point in the shift and the letting go process you awaken to an easier way. You are learning now that there is an easier way than working. Yes as you first attract things, then you manifest things. Then as you let go and surrender to what and who you are, then it becomes easier still. All you have to do is synchronize with love and let your Divine Self guide you through inspiration and then lead you to You the Creator. Yes, there is an easier way still but it is a transition that you can practice and attain a higher state. Otherwise the properties cannot open and evolve. As you see, the miracle workers can do this temporarily and go back to the old ways. Eventually you will reach a split in the journey where you will not need the old ways and take the road called LET GO."

"Yes, it is easy and simple but not until your knowing has shifted—knowing without doubt, condition or fear and living fully in the heart."

Learning to be responsible

"Responsibility is a very major part of the transition as it begins to change through the stages that are as you had determined. These stages are Sleeping, Awakening, Awakened, Expanded, Enlightened and Ascended. The process of letting go and manifestation are related to this evolution."

*"In the process of **Attraction**, you realize you are creating energies that attract like energies so you begin to take responsibility for what you are generating. M**anifestation** is the next level where you realize you are creating the external experiences in all situations and you begin to take responsibilities. At the **Co-creation** stage, you realize that you are creating the perceptions of everything in your life and that it is all within you so you take responsibility for all energies created regardless of whose energies they are. At*

Materialization, *you realize that you are creating the physical world as your hologram and you take full responsibility for the movie you are playing. Finally, at* **Creation,** *you realize you are part of it all and that you are the One guiding all of Creation."*

"Let us speak of bliss for a moment. What if you could go into bliss as you sit? Let us say you know what bliss is. It is the wonderful joy you feel at certain moments. This may be after something you desire suddenly becomes real to you, when you are in love and you touch, or when you have perceived a lack that suddenly becomes abundance, someone is healed, when two people unite physically during a climax. There is an instant feeling of bliss that radiates around you—and it does indeed radiate! Let us suppose you could sit and create this feeling continuously. Would you leave your chair?"

"You may say but I must get up and pay the bills, go to work, feed the children. What if you paid the bills by knowing the bank account is full? You don't need to work; you can sit there to infinity feeling this energy of bliss. Try placing yourself here and imagine what you would do? Yes, we know this is not an easy concept—you think of an addiction to drugs and others would perceive you as a lost cause—but not if all of your perceived responsibilities were taken care of because you could truly co-create."

"Even a more difficult transition is the one of knowing it is all a hologram of your design. What if you knew that you and your soul mate were actually sitting in a parallel dimension as your etheric Higher Selves watching the two of you in the movie. They were sipping a cosmic cocktail laughing and wondering what you would do next—what you would perceive, and what you would learn from the next events that were planned? They are you know. But none of this will make sense until you

truly "Let go" of the world you create and have created, which is not only an energy field of perceptions and experience in and from the world that enfolds you, but that you have created as the hologram that appears to be solid and real. Yes, it is indeed a difficult shift. But that is the way of it and by transisting this will become more and more of the knowing within you that becomes impossible for anyone or anything to dislodge."

"But before we leave the idea of whether you would sit there all day, we will answer the question for you. You would not sit there intoxicated with bliss that comes from memories because you would want to seek out new bliss that you have not yet had from inspiration. In one state you do not let go but in the next you let go. That is what the physical hologram is all about. Now if you knew it was a big show then what value would there be in the show and experience? Would you play the roles the same way? Think about this as it is a major dividing line and where there is a split in your journey."

"Your journey is marked with these signposts of Sleeping, Awakening, Awakened, Expanded, Ascended. And the process that unfolds is holding onto 3D to letting go of 3D as well as following the transition of the four laws of energy. These signposts are there when your awareness changes otherwise they do not reveal themselves. You will reach a split where it says 'Let Go' and 'Hold On'."

"We say this because there are certain transformations that occur in your evolution back to the Higher Self and the Light Being you are. These are the various glimpses of a new reality such as the instant miracles and these unexplainable things that come. But as the process unfolds along the path, these abilities of telepathy, instant healing, energy sensing, levitation, reading the temporary energies of others (psychic); all of these things that have been frowned on in your science and

society begin to surface in you as you begin to bring these to you in others and other situations. You are drawing these, attracting, and manifesting them around you and in yourself. As these develop and the awareness of the reality of them solidifies in your beliefs and actions remember you are attaining more light and begin to realize these things we speak of. To be an Interdimensional being, Co-creator all of this will accelerate your journey once you see glimpses of this new reality. At some point the split will occur and the hologram will be meaningless and senseless because the game you set up is revealed."

"*That is what your game is about. How do you as a creator and a wonderful love filled Being of Light create new, unexperienced bliss that a physical body, and physical world allow, without polarity and without the body. Yes, indeed it is an interesting question. You will need to let go to know.*"

Changing beliefs

"*Yes, belief and life are interchangeable as one is the other. Sit and repeat a thought over and over and you will imbed this into your life habits. Conduct a habit over and over and it will form a belief. Say you simply begin to try a new action like meditating or a walk in the woods. This is a spontaneous thing that you heard about so you do it for some supposed benefits. You either continue it or you don't. If you do, your belief begins to shift as you begin to encode this into your belief as worthy, beneficial, and rewarding. The activity creates and shifts the belief. The other way is to reverse this and start with the belief. You simply believe this will be great and so you do it. Now the belief shifts the activity and in fact reinforces the belief. In both cases the same thing is achieved. The belief system changes.*"

"Test your beliefs. Sit down in a quiet place and just focus on your breathing—in and out deeper and quieter. Then ask your Higher Self: 'Higher Self does Ed believe in miracles?' What is the first thing that pops into your mind. The answer may be there before you even finish the question. Don't look to analyze this. It will not be a voice or anything dramatic. It will be a simple yes or no that is simply a thought surfacing instantly. That is the truth of it. Don't think it was something you did not want to hear. Think about changing habits or belief to get a yes answer. A belief changes when you make it so."

"Outside changes inside and inside changes outside. Make your choice but create the intent/action. Belief is a result of many things but primarily your experiences which are recorded in the hologram. The brain is the control center of the hologram and is itself the hologram. Events, action, others, senses all become processed by this center to give you a perception of all that is in your hologram. This is a process by which a perception forms your belief and habits. What is of note is that most lives are surrounded by a surrender to polarity, to egos, and to other beliefs—yes from those that you have attracted or created in your hologram. No wonder it is a reinforcement of what you believe, is it not? Let go and this changes as your responsibility shifts from what you have created, or are creating, or what you memories perceive, and zero this out. Then a new belief system can enter and habitualize itself. Then that begins to attract and manifest more of the likeness of it. As you let go through the beliefs and habits with limits, you zero out and enter a realm with no limits."

"Yes, learn to let it be and practice the peace and letting go we told you about. It will simply evolve. You may live as a hermit or monk but that is not what we want you to do. We prefer you retain your qualities and become an example of how the spirit and the body can merge so you can show and lead others."

More on the nature of holograms

"Imagine this: You and your spouse are sitting in some cosmic chair, sipping a cosmic cocktail. This is a funny scene because you are in your other form as an etheric energy form of consciousness—like the one that goes on a vacation when you have an Out of Body or a Near Death Experience. The two of you are watching a movie of your physical selves below."

"As you learn to let go the hologram in your mind simply remains in virtual suspension, along with everything that is in it. All are suspended and as you quicken to this and realize your powers, you will change, rearrange, materialize at will but only when vibration is above a threshold. At some point, the create stage becomes instant and the complete hologram can be changed as you would in a day dream where you can see or feel anything imaginable. This will take some time to get used to. It will be like making your own movies and entering them."

"As you further detach from old energy, the excitement will begin to turn inward as you look to divine desires rather than 3D human ones. This is because ego is fading in its grip as you take on the trust and faith that you will create whatever you need or that we will protect and nurture you. This is not a simple transition as one has been so trained to only have faith in themselves and trust no one. It will be confusing to many and the old ways will not be released to the ways of faith and trust."

"Concentrate on these. Learn your new senses as they awaken. Let the skill evolve naturally but always pay attention to their existence and their evolution. They will only become stronger if you acknowledge them and place your attention on them. You will begin to feel different—lighter, fuller, shinier, happier, content, more confident in knowing the truth of us and yourself. Your

sense will strengthen and be more united with us as we learn to communicate automatically."

"You wonder how there can be a world with no darkness. We are in a world where darkness exists but not within us. Your world can be the same, and although darkness can grow as the light is withdrawn, it cannot exist where the purpose is to shine light on it, not to nurture or create more. Anyone who ascends may purposely descend or be drawn, yes. No one can control the will of others here and even though you may not believe this in your world, it is so. So for us it does not exist as it is indeed of lower vibration and we simply shine a higher vibration upon it to eliminate or recycle it."

"If you were in a dark cave where you knew that by extinguishing your light, you would become a victim of the dark would you strive to keep it lit? And if you knew that that light could bring you wondrous things to maintain peace, love and harmony with all things, would you extinguish it? If the concept of polarity and greed and hate is but a distant memory of what is inappropriate to your and other's life, would you encourage it to live by you giving it life? And when others know about a struggle with dark that may be coming upon you, would you not see that awareness bring assistance?"

"Of course, there is no absolute guarantee that the heaven on earth shall be eternal. Remember that you are all creating your world now and will be in going forward. And remember you are of free will. So will you as ascended beings fall to the dark again? It is an interesting speculation but we have not seen such happenings when the final stage of ascension is reached. And when such ascension can provide for you anything that can be imagined, would you purposely set out to manifest dark energies? As a part of the creator, will you create conflict and destruction when you have worked so

hard not to? We truly cannot answer this as it is part of evolution."

"Polarity, greed and conflict do not exist here any more that ice can exist in a world of fire. Certainly one can bring the ice into the fire, but it cannot remain in that lower state. Hatred cannot exist in a space filled with love and light. Disease and dis-ease cannot live here as well. This does not mean that it cannot change and that an ascended one cannot fall back but we see this as highly unlikely and not a model within our cosmos— certainly not one governed by God and not one where the individuals clearly understand they are creators."

"You ask us about the holograms. Yes they are. Both are holograms. How do they interact you ask. Let us look at what you are familiar with—your movies which you can stack on a shelf. They are frames you call pictures, each one being a representation of an instant in time. They have no meaning or emotion to anyone until they are viewed frame after frame, now after now, each representing a replacement in your time of the other. By your viewing them in sequence, they present you with experience, emotion, feelings and even physical sensations. Yet they are nothing until you view them."

"Each *movie sitting on the shelf has no time. Each frame sitting in your computer can be modified and changed, or the sequence rearranged at someone's will—even you if you created that movie. "*

"So let us say you created many movies. One was done in Mexico near the ocean. One was done in the jungles of Africa. One was done in the desert. And one was done at home with family. So in your movies, you choose players. In the movies you have on the shelf these are actors and they can be in many movies at the same instant in time can they not. You and your players can be as well. Who you choose to place in your movies is up

to you and they are in fact replicated if you want. Perhaps they are different characters but nevertheless the same person."

"The place is the setting. It is your atomic world that appears real as the movie is created. Yet it is the same world on film. Each of the players is within that physical world. What if these worlds existed in parallel? And you were the producer who chose the actors and the settings? What if these segments or frames or 'nows' were all sitting in a virtual space that your mind could access, string together, experience, or modify instantly by simply rearranging the frames or changing the pictures? Or perhaps rearranging the electrons into an new atomic configuration?"

"What if you could simply suspend time by stopping the movie and entering a new one? The old one can be started from where it left off or it can be changed at will. And when you desire to view the other, you stop the new one and come back to the first."

"This is similar to how a hologram is created and how you interact with it. At the level of higher vibration this is the way things are. It is natural and all commanded by conscious awareness. This is the way your different lives have been created and recorded as experience in your emotional body. They are all evolving at different rates or they have been played out. They are all 'nows' in a virtual sea of experiences. And they can all be accessed, re-experienced, or even changed at will."

On thoughts-what they are

"Thoughts are everywhere, a wave of electrons looking for mates. They come from everything and everywhere as a sea of life spawning itself in the cosmos. They look to grow and mate and expand and become I AM. Sit down and put your mind onto something and a thought

comes forward. Where from? Is it from you or is it from something else? Is it what you attracted or is it what is attracting you. It is a sea of no thing consciousness. Change your focus—another thought?"

"Words images, emotion, they are all the same as you focus on them and put attention to them. They all have a signature and you tune into these like a TV or radio. Then you control the strength of these using the amplifier to add feeling, words, images. These are amplifiers and creators of purpose placed into the energy stream. These thoughts are seeking a mate and to grow into something beautiful to expand the Universe."

"All life desires to live, expand and flourish. Thoughts are no different. Each who receives one has a different interpretation or perception of its meaning. It is a vibrational signature like a word, image, but your interpretation and the emotion it creates is unique. Thoughts are independent of language. Each has an interpreter that converts it to a familiar language. Thoughts can be sent by focus or they can be loose of focus and wander aimlessly. They, upon life given by you as a creator, look to fulfill their destiny which is to live, grow, expand thereby seeking out its mate—a likeness of its signature. It is not a positive or negative, it is simply a likeness that fulfills itself—as you seek your soul mate which is a division of you."

"We create thoughts like anything else. It is given strength by your energy generators in your body. Its influence is determined by the emotional bodies' strength. It can be forgotten or lost but it never disappears as each has a tag identifying it as yours or whoever created it. All things have these but not all can create like you."

"Thoughts are an expression of consciousness to focus awareness (attention) on something. They are an

expression of Creation at the first level. Note how if you think a certain way, you will attract others or be attracted to others that have similar thoughts and behaviors. This is not a coincidence. The thoughts are working to express themselves and work with you since they are your creation. They like to grow, expand and to do this they need to be vitalized in strength. This is through adding other vibrations such as images, words and feeling—adding the power of the emotional body. These then become actions, plans, materialization as you have surmised. Yes, it is the steps of attraction, manifestation, co-creation and materialization. It all works together. At a higher level of vibration thoughts can become instant attractors and manifestors like in a daydream. At a higher level the same can be done in the 3D world which we refer to as co-creation and materialization but eventually when you understand you are the creator speaking, it does not require the co."

"What are they? They are vibrations set in motion and given life. They have no language any more than audio signatures can be interpreted by a variety of devices. You all have an instant interpreter but there can be misguidance in some messages when the translation occurs—like when your computers translate languages. They may change meaning and the perception of what they mean and how they affect you can vary. Thoughts are the base of living creation made of electrons, the base of all that is."

Setting out your desires

"We see that you have set up your manifesting desires and your mantras. We are pleased to see that you are claiming you are an interdimensional being of light and not subject to time. Yes, it is so, we are not subject to time and in the ascended world there is none. We do suggest that you set up your desires with some modifications using symbology and writing these out."

"First, you should clearly set out your heart's desires by writing these down. Set up your key words to represent these. For example you had Zero Point as one and miracles as another. For each of these the word can be assigned like a mantra that triggers the desire and intent instantly and you can then assign a symbol to all of these. When you write these, add how your desire would make your emotional body glow with vibrations."

"Every day for three days, you should read these out loud and as you read them repeat the key word three times to associate this with the word, or better still visualize the symbol. The symbol you seemed to choose was the two triangles on each other forming a six pointed star encircled. This is fine, yes it is the star of David and an alchemical representation of divine."

"After three days, simply visualize the six pointed star before night and you can do this again in the morning when you awaken. If you need to modify the words then modify the segment in writing again and repeat this for three days again."

"You will find that this allows you to set the action and intent as you would in the no time world—instantly."

"Yes, you are indeed learning to be a multidimensional by your symbols and words as you have stated. It is a start of how the mind can multitask in parallel and respond automatically. It is as we do it. You are already doing this at night—you struggle with it in the day as you see no 3D representation or evidence of the work. It is happening, however, at its own pace as your body is not as quickly adjustable as your mind is. This means that over the next period, an adjustment in your sensory systems will change as the light being part begins to unfold in you."

"This means that your senses will change as your sight begins to see energy outlines in other things. Your hearing will expand to pick up subtle energy vibrations, your sense of knowing will improve. You will begin to pick up thoughts, smell energies and sense them as being positive or negative, read other's energy being held for manifestation, your sense of feel and touch will expand as invisible world begins to make more sense so to speak and it begins to overshadow the usual material world sensory system. This is the light body and the etheric energy of your duplicate that is now evolving from the heart to overshadow the 3D outer body. It is the next stage to evolving teleportation and telepathy and materialization like in the dream state. We acknowledge that this is a large transition and it is not an instant process in most. It will lead you into a new time space without limitations."

"How do you do this? Place attention to the development of this light body and opening its abilities. Attention, trust, faith and belief—then patience. In your meditation, ask it to be so and place attention on the heart and the completion."

"Why is it so difficult for you? Your roots in 3D are still in the material world-it will pass suddenly when you least expect it."

Rid yourself of analysis

"You are very busy looking for analytical things like steps, reasons, processes and results. These logical left brain activities are interfering with what has no process or time. While you seek, you lose sight of the fundamental process of which there is none. It is a matter of releasing this and letting it be as it is in a natural way—it is this process that is your conundrum of limitation. You impose conditions, expectations, limits on how this works, steps where there are none."

"Let go of this and enfold the desire of being enjoyed, the emotion of joy fulfilled being part of the emotional body. It is what you must do to surround your need with feelings and emotion. That is it. Can you stop thinking, analyzing and inspecting things? Can you let go and really let others do the job? And trust that it is done? Can you thank someone before you see the job done? Can you love the outcome without any conditions attached?"

"Let go of steps and procedure. Place attention yes, let go without expectation or signs of correctness. Look at these words that you analyze of detach, unconditional, faith, trust, gratitude, feeling. What do they mean to you? Is your perception of these limiting you?"

Can you let go of what you know
Can you open up and let no thing flow
Can you just be in only NOW
Go inside, let the heart show how

HOLOGRAMS | REALITY

What if I create all I think and feel
What if it's a movie I believe is real
And what I believed is what is not
Would I then change the plot?

Now that I have introduced these holograms of reality, I want to give you some communications that came to me about how we form reality. The idea that we create and live in a Star Trek type hologram was difficult to believe. What this set of communications does however, is shed light on the science conundrum and actually gives some credibility to the "art" of quantum physics.

You live in a living intelligent hologram

"You have holograms on your mind. Yes you live in and create a hologram for the purpose of your experience. Think back to our sessions on manifesting and co-creation and the practice of materialization. Remember how you give life to a thought or action or feeling. It is by a dual projection and reflection of images from the mind's eye."

"You are creating energy that will either seek out an energy mate or it will materialize into something that the energy represents into a new form. It is made up from the essence of particles of what consciousness is made up of—electrons you call them—common to all things

whether material or non material. This is what you call a reality, the attention of your awareness within the total consciousness—the mind of God. Each energy lives and has purpose and once created, lives to expand itself according to its purpose and its design which will behave according to cosmic laws of creation. Once alive, it remains so and evolves as it was perceived at the time of creation. Then it grows, changes and evolves."

"Think also of how we have informed you of materialization. Think how you form the holographic image of some thing that can materialize. It then needs alignment with the divine partner. It is with the approval to actually create knowing the divine cosmic laws and being are explicitly in the heart."

"Each particle is of the whole and all is one therefore all that exists, existed or will exist resides here in the hologram which is the mind—the total consciousness of the One—the Creator. In your lower form of mind and body, this becomes like an individual compartment of the whole which is your local individual consciousness."

"Once thoughts or action of the Lower form create, these energies remain to attain their purpose. They may be transmuted if you have attained the level of vibration that is of the Higher Body and Mind. However, this responsibility is not of the lower form. If the energies are created from the Lower Self, they will simply congeal into a transitional etheric state, attract, evolve and interact as designed by intent and attention. It fulfills its cosmic purpose assigned by you the creator."

"Through your senses of the Lower Self, the experiences are interpreted and perceived with the brain being the interpreter. The mind is what creates, sets, and interprets, the instructions and is the actual link and control center of all this interacting energy and the body which itself is energy. A body is thus a hologram formed

the same way and once created, a genetic code is set creating a signature of its makeup as in the DNA. It is the blueprint than can replicate and evolve once given life."

All energy is alive and expanding

"Let us continue on the hologram and you. In the strictest sense, the consciousness of the Creator of the One is like a holograph with some major difference. Describing it this way is a convenient way for you to relate to it and understand it. It reflects all that can be or has ever been imagined by God. It is not a true hologram in your scientific terms however, in that it is a living and intelligent medium with all that exists; living and interacting within it—all energies—living things that are themselves seeking to expand, flourish and ascend towards their purposes in their own individualized consciousness. Flowers, animals, human, rocks, all energy placed within this hologram in their lower forms seek to evolve and expand through their instincts and purposes as encoded in their DNA or life code and their higher states of expression. In humans the expression of this is through Higher Self which itself is consciousness."

"At the fundamental stage, all things are energy of consciousness and all have some form of consciousness as individualized. This brings and records an awareness through various processing of other energies—or sensory systems—to interact with and to seek expression and to evolve in a way to find their purposes. This is a cycle of material form—material by perception—of being created, living, blossoming, reproducing and all things are drawn to this process as encoded in the DNA as directed by their consciousness. In your lower form of Self, you are no different than a flower or rock or animal that seeks to live life, flourish, expand, and reproduce. You like all else are able to reproduce and create and evolve within an

interactive, live world of the hologram which itself is also evolving and live."

"You as a higher being can also create energy with your mind and body by placing attention here and triggering energy systems. You give it life and set it loose to evolve according to purpose—given by you if so defined or by cosmic laws of evolution and expression."

"Your Lower Self is designed to interpret energies so as to process them through senses and interpret them according to your brain. This is sensed by the body and transmitted back into it for action-reaction, as well as recorded in consciousness for the perception of experience. It is so it can learn, grow, live, and expand according to instinct (lower purpose), cosmic law and expand (higher purpose). This process of material physical perception is this way and once some thing is formed in the hologram, it remains as part of it for others to perceive and sense."

"In the lower form all interacts with and reacts to these energies that form the group or global hologram. Although you are creating certain energies through your mind and equipment, these are transient energies not yet congealed and are given life to seek purpose and find energy mates or entrain with like energies in the hologram. These energies can be dark or light and depending on their creation can do this rapidly or remain forever within the hologram."

"In the Higher form, however, you are able to create new energies, passing the temporarily congealed state and materialize directly from the total consciousness—as a creator. This is where a huge difference lies in the ability to transmute or actually create within the hologram."

A new 5D hologram is forming

"We continue on the hologram that you live in. It has been so for much time and you were given entry to this world of Creator's mind and consciousness. This was created as a wondrous Eden of beauty and perfection within which beings could live, expand and learn to love and enjoy the life they had been given."

"The entry of beings to this world has not gone according to an evolution of the higher state. Beings take on a lower state and have the choice of free will. Many retain the lower energy states due to their own designs and needs. Essentially many other negative energies have been given life and purpose, evolving not within the light. As a result, the hologram of consciousness has many interacting forces and energies not of the light. Energies you create retain a signature of ownership to find energy that it itself vibrates or entrains with. It draws other energies that represent people, situations, and their owners with them. Thus in the hologram energies live and interact. All beings interact in these physical and non-physical energies playing out their lives, as you do."

"Many times this has resulted in much darkness within the hologram accumulating in a temporary form attempting to congeal into the hologram, not yet mated. It has dominated and at times almost destroyed the hologram. And so it has come to its end of a natural cycle of life as well at which point the energies are transmuted by death or by active awareness of its purpose. This purpose, to many of you, is known and therefore you have begun to form a new hologram in parallel which represents a world different than this one. The process is not known as to how these two worlds will merge or separate except to say it is all at and end which is the beginning."

The 3D and 5D holograms will merge

"The hologram you have formed for yourself has been limited through your beliefs. As that changes, your senses and awareness of it expands, and then you begin to take control of it. As this occurs, the new 5D hologram that has been formed—much like your global consciousness—begins to be clearer. As your limited senses of 3D intent bring material and mental perceptions of experience, so does the 5D self do the same in the new hologram. These worlds then expand so you will experience either at will. You are learning to use 5D senses in a 3D world. You will bring 3D into the 5D world."

"As you sit quietly and imagine a world, or write about it, you are forming your hologram with your signature. This is a part of the larger hologram of joint imaginations. Anything is possible here but you are not yet able to walk this world except in your imagination. Once you give life to it, it is there and it can be changed as in a movie. All vibrations here are above a threshold, all is interlinked and your awareness of how this works in one medium of intelligent evolving life unfolds to you. This you do not understand but there are cosmic laws that govern the way energies evolve, interact and change. This you will learn soon."

The 4D hologram is a transition plane

"Your mind is busy with 4D as part of the hologram. Yes, it is another plane or dimension which is all around you like the air you breathe. It is beyond your 3D sensory system bounds, however—which you have imposed on yourself. It is where energy is first created and interacts at an invisible etheric level. It is like a transition stage where energy waits in some form awaiting congealment and purpose. It is there to seek out an energy mate, to

congeal, to materialize, or to co-create some thing that it is or represents. Think back to the laws and how you create energies that seek mates."

"For example, you may have a moment when you are angry and your thoughts, and emotions instantly form this transition energy in the 4D plane. It is created in your field of influence. What does it do? It is tagged as belonging to you as you created it. Under cosmic law it has been created with a purpose of your anger that enfolded it. This may or may not be clear or strong in its intent provided by you. Under cosmic law, it is a living energy with purpose and such purpose must strive to satisfy by seeking out a likeness to it and its purpose— an energy mate. It is a living energy seeking to expand and satisfy its purpose and signature vibration that it represents—namely your anger. So it can do this in several ways."

"It can find a likeness to attract a situation that satisfies the purpose by an experience. It manifests a balance. It manifests, it evolves, it seeks until this is done and balanced so the purpose is released. Such energy, depending upon its strength and clarity can take unknown time and it can also influence other energy fields to have an effect on other's fields. It must do this in order to draw other energies to it. So it may be something that is in your own field that is strong enough to affect dysfunction in your own field and body because it is attached to you—and your belief system can attract others the same way. The dysfunction remains until it is balanced, like the idea of karma. But many times the energy results in creating disease or dis-ease or dysfunction in your Lower Self. The effect of regression reveals the imbalance to correct this. Many energies are created dark troublesome energies without purpose and they will simply be around looking for something dark to attach to."

"The 4D world is full of these energies and over centuries have accumulated much unbalanced energy that has not yet satisfied its purpose and these affect the larger consciousness of those living in the hologram—in 3D. Once this was cleansed of darkness that accumulated over centuries—cleansed by Archangel Michael and his Angels but it has accumulated again."

"You see that energy can be poorly defined and without purpose, unable to balance. It can be anything imaginable and there is no time here so it stays in 4D."

"Your higher abilities if developed—as with clairvoyants and psychics—are able to read these energies and sense them with expanded senses. They can read these living energies to detect the owner's purposes, and strength. This allows them to have visions, and read information that is attached to them as well as their owners. They can reveal what is forming or attached to you transcending past or future as the senses pick up this information thereby reading the future or revealing the past. They can see, hear, feel, read, and know what is forming, the strength, and the purpose."

"Yes, ghosts, apparitions, dark energies, boogey men of unimaginable purposes and creations reside here. But you have been protected from these by your sensory limitations."

"You have not yet widened the range of your sensory systems to read these energies—and to see them. Many animals have shown example of enhanced ranges that sense these energies—much beyond yours. You do have them and they must be awakened again in your 3D form. In your 5D form there are many more as there are in your 4D form which is your aura that surrounds your body. You have others awaiting your awakening."

"So yes there are many energy forms here awaiting their own evolution and purpose. That is why we speak of 3D and 5D, and not of 4D as 4D is simply a transition hologram from one to the other."

"What you sow is what you reap reflects this 4D hologram of transition from one to another or back to the one that created it. It reflects the cosmic workings of energy as you sow it in 4D to reap it in 3D from where it is sown—or use it to grow to 5D. But you may not know what this is, and how or when it shall reap—that is part of raising your vibrations to sow wonderful positive energy in every moment and to detect and balance that which is attached."

Materializing and attracting in 3D and 4D

"Recall what we told you about materialization. We said: Again, it is attention and intention and love as the substance of power that allows an image to congeal into a material representation of an object in a hologram. This means that the Divine Mind be the total agent of the image of some object that is simply created in your mind's eye. It will be a clear image so you need much practice here. At the point at which your Higher Mind and the Heart—the congealer—create that image. It is projected onto a place of choice by intent and at the same time the image of the mind is projected to the God Source of the One to be reflected back like a mirror as a beam of divine light to the same place of choice—yes it is like converging laser beams of light."

"As these two actions converge upon the place of choice from you and the divine beam from the source, they form a holographic duplicate representation of the object that is to be replicated or materialized. Yes, from a wave form to an atomic form as the electrons arrange themselves into the image which is your higher

consciousness choosing a new possibility from the no thing."

"No, you do not concern yourself as to how the chemistry, atomic structure and so one occurs as it is all under natural cosmic law that such an arrangement is created. These laws understand how this is done and your divine consciousness abides by these. So they all understand what this is made up of, to congeal this into the expression of the holographic image, to be interpreted as such by your and other sensory systems of your brain—your sensory receiving stations."

"You first create a clear image in your mind's eye with the assistance of the heart, then project it to a place of materialization. Then you project this to the One to project back to the same place. A holographic image is created. This is similar to the way a holographic image is created with beams of light that are split, reflected and converged again. What is it? A hologram? What form is it? It is whatever you see clearly that your brain understands and has meaning for or memory of."

"It is your brain that does the final work as a material representation by retrieving what it knows and what cosmic rules apply in the material representation. It retrieves information and the cosmic rule simply "knows" what it is."

"So let us say an apple is chosen. Is it big, small, red, yellow? What kind is it? The brain is designed to hold its own local knowledge—like a copy of its own experience that is held current. It uses this to fill the gaps of creating this from what it knows about the apple. The brain, and of course your consciousness or mind has information and the cosmic rules of its composition, formation, are drawn to complete the picture."

"So a word, an object, an image all have meaning to the brain by its experience and with the assistance of cosmic law reverse engineers the process to create the result from memory and let us call it technical information as to its composition or material makeup. Although an image of the apple is only a representation in your lower mind and brain, it already has the appropriate material characteristics from higher sources as to how it would be materialized. So anything can indeed happen in materialization therefore it requires a high degree of responsibility."

"You see, the brain which interprets senses also fills in the gaps to complete it. Many times, you will not actually see things exactly, as the brain only picks up half of what is there, filling in the rest by itself—unless you place strict attention on it and see the difference. The brain fills the gaps, holes, missing information and uses a process you call extrapolate and interpolate from its memory what is needed to complete the picture. If you see and read the words "I luv yu" or "wht a wndrful da" you know what this is meaning, do you not? Your brain is interpolating the true meaning even though parts are missing. But by closer inspection and attention, you see the difference. So it is with an image of an apple."

"The brain is the holographic processor that creates the meaning, composition, and representation through its memory and the interpretation of the senses of your lower body. You see, feel, and taste an apple and it seems so real. So if you take the senses of see, feel, taste and the memories of this, then reverse engineer the process back through the brain—with divine assistance—it will create the apple as appearing solid in the hologram."

"What you have not done is to do this outside of your imagination in an eyes open conscious state of awareness. Yet as you know, some can indeed do this—

like holy men—by a reverse process which is easy in your mind but not in your hologram of 3D. But you are learning. It is what you are learning as your vibration reaches a certain level. Yes, this is so because of a certain level of responsibility, and partnership with the higher self and the Divine is required as reflected by the alignment of heart, purpose and Divinity—the One."

"Recall also how we spoke of the laws of attraction and manifestation in the hologram. Yes, this is how energy is formed in the 4D world of the hologram to seek out its purpose."

Congealing energies

"We shall continue on holograms. You can understand that there is much energy being created by all beings on earth. Some is dark, some is of the light, some is weak, some is strong, some has purpose some has not. But without exception each energy formed is attached to the creator and joins the collective coalescing energy. It is important to understand that in creating it, a tag is placed upon it—a word, a vision, an image, a symbol that represents this so it can be recalled for further attention instantly. It can be made clear, stronger, enforced, reinforced and defined with clarity and strength of emotion so it is a stronger vibration energy with a clear purpose. Otherwise it can be aimless and purposeless with no thing to do except to bring unto itself the same, likeness—for you the creator of it—to experience. Clarity of purpose, strength of vibration through continued attention makes it strong and powerful to entrain and attract that which it reflects and is its purpose."

"You understand that all beings form a collective hologram the same way as a composite of individual ones. These are combined as the group hopes, wishes, actions and perceptions all the time interacting and

congealing into various forms that may materialize into new energies and forms. It is within this vast hologram that yours exists all being within the larger one of the One—the mind of God. The hologram itself is alive and all within it cannot be changed in its perceived material form—a joint belief and congealment of form—without the attention and agreement of the Higher Divine Mind—your link to the Creator of the One. This is as you know requires the higher vibration and purpose reflecting the truth of your essence of light. Otherwise energies only attract and attach to each other while at the same time that which is perceived to be material and physical in the 3D dimension remain unaltered except by its own growth evolution."

"Thus there are interacting layers in the hologram of the One—3D material world, 4D coalescing energies, 5D etheric world. Within this 3D hologram layer all that is material is therefore your own holographic plane as perceived by you. What you perceive from it is your parallel world and yours alone interacting with the 3D world forming your physical hologram of your reality. It is recorded and once attention goes there it remains."

So what is all this pointing to? No thing or nothing is a state of consciousness that has not formed any thing yet. It must therefore be everything as it forms a reality by conscious attention to some thing. Hmmmmm.

A Being of Light you are indeed
Its third eye to project material in need
Ask the Divine heart to its image reflect
New reality materializes as they intersect

LOWER | HIGHER

The issue of mine is bills to pay
I work and save for a rainy day
How can there be an easier way
To know the bills are paid and play

What are they telling us? The choices you make, the perceptions you create, the beliefs you hold, and the way you relate to all that exists, creates the life you live. Absolutely everything you see, hear, feel, read, and sense are perceptions of your experience that create living energy. These draw more of the same to you. These are dependent on how you alone manage your mind to decide what these energies are. That is it.

And as of this time, there is no scientific explanation for how this works. But do you really care? Do you want to spend a lifetime or a decade like me seeking the answers? Can you afford that? Over 90% of humans believe in a God or a Higher Power. Do they support their belief with an endless quest for scientific proof? I don't think so. Do you believe in a Higher Power? Do you believe in incarnation? Do you really care what others tell you about your belief in this area? Those who believe have **Let Go** of that silly quest for proof and simply believe it is so. This strange pursuit of scientific proof is relegated to the few, not the many—yet it seems that the few influence the beliefs of the many. And the mind, that wonderful, invisible field of energy, that thing made of no thing that governs your life is simply there creating your consciousness and awareness.

So what have we learned about this energy and how it is influenced? It seems to be wrapped up in more invisible no things that cannot be explained, engaging words like surrender, into the heart, beliefs, trust, faith, letting go and many other words that can be argued about forever as to what they mean and why they are important in taking a new stance. And then there is the question of how they have any relevance to creating a better life for you.

So with respect to miracles, manifesting, co-creation, materialization, there are three points that need to be repeated:

- Science cannot and will not explain miracles, consciousness, the mind and co-creation. So why waste time imposing limits that come from that inadequacy?
- The mind is the block to the doorway to what science cannot explain. So why continue to fill it with things that maintain the block?
- The world is full of unexplainable happenings that can dramatically shift your mind and life into unimaginable bliss. So why not fill the mind with these experiences?

No thing will ever become some thing unless you break down this barrier of belief. No-one can do it but you. All of these words and actions such as surrender, faith, trust, compassion, oneness, forgiveness have a meaning in thought, action and form—all simple energies. But the key here is what these mean to you. It is your thoughts about the meaning of these that give energy to your beliefs. It is your beliefs that give the actions of these to the way you perceive and live your life.

It is your perceptions that create the energy. Is it so difficult to believe that absolutely everything in your movie of life creates a *perception* in you that can affect your life? Is it so hard to believe that every one of these could be *perceived* differently by anyone else and that any one of these can create an experience of feeling in you? Is it so hard to believe that everything is a form of vibrating energy? Can you stretch out, leave the traditional science beliefs behind and accept that even you can control, change and even create any of these energies—even the physical?

Dropping into the heart to let go

You may have detected the personal quest of mine that began as a need to understand why my life was the way it was and why others had lives so different. I could not understand why others had fame and riches while I slogged the gopher wheel of life encountering disappointment after disappointment. What began as a scientific mission was the journey but with its disappointments. I wanted to know why I—little ol' me—could not create miracles like many others. The journey simply led to the inadequacies of science and technology until I began to realize it was that quest that carried the doubt that limited me.

This fact let new information in. I simply s*urrendered* to the fact that what I thought was truth was not. So I let go of it and its limits, simply having the *faith* that a solution—not the problem—would come. My *belief* simply became one of openness to whatever came and that indeed there were limitless possibilities to a better life. I simply had to create the energy of intent and let it find my solution in an infinite realm of possibilities.

Was it hard? Yes. I was in business, programmed like a robo-executive towards assets, performance, budgets, business plans, and all those rules, laws, limits of science and technology that so many are under. There was no instant revelation. There was no instant ability to pay the bills. There was no instant change in life style. But here was an instant in time where my mind understood that there was a need to reprogram it a certain way. There was no magic silver bullet but there was a belief that perhaps bills could be paid a new way.

It was not difficult to understand after the work and research I did that letting go of science was no big deal. And the gaps were being filled by many of the messages that gave me more insight on how this energy worked. In early 2010 I decided to go to our Sanctuary in Africa and practice what I preached. This was my "boot camp" for Letting Go. After all, talk is easy. Could I, the enlightened one really do all these unexplainable things with energy that I wrote about? In a nutshell, the story that evolved was about my Higher and Lower Self. Who did I have learn to let go to? My Higher Self. Here is what they said.

Let us tell you of letting go

"Letting go does not mean to suddenly drop your responsibilities. It simply changes the way and nature of them. As you realize everything that exists is One, you begin to create a transformation in you."

"Your Higher Mind begins to be with you constantly in the foreground not the background. It is indeed with you always but because it is of a higher plane, it becomes crowded by more aggressive, Lower Mind activities. These are the constant thoughts of what you must do in your world—go to work, pay the bill instead of what you would like to do—the heart's desire and inspirational activities common to the Higher Mind. So it may never speak except faintly making suggestions to your thought process, overshadowed by more active lower vibration

mind where ego controls creating consciousness of needs and responsibilities to live and protect."

"As the shift occurs, the higher mind brings in the higher thoughts of higher vibration as its peace, love, compassion for all enfolds your life actions. Your perceptions begin to shift to a higher perspective. It is the same as you follow thoughts now but the shift is one of following new thoughts. This is like what you have written about; creating new habits to break old habits—a new way of thinking, hence belief of the Higher Mind."

"There is also a progression here. The thought-action-belief-habit-chore-discord-fear process of the Lower Mind is the tendency if the ego and Lower Mind are not managed. The discord turns to fear with the preoccupation of the worry about the future and responsibilities, as based upon what had happened in the past."

"Recall the sleeping, attraction, manifestation, co-creation, creation laws. This process shifts at a certain stage where the lower mind is let go and the higher mind prevails. As this changes, the shift moves from what you must do (work, pay bills) to what you desire or would like to do (passion). As this changes and the laws unfold, this changes from paying those bills and the worry and attention towards these perceptions of responsibility. It shifts to the new way of creative spiritual powers that know the bills are taken care of. It is belief of the material needs that limit the spiritual powers of being the Co-creator."

"This becomes stronger as the Higher Mind evolves to its rightful place to become the new command center, the place it resides in as the heart—the Graceland you call it connected to everything through the no thing."

"As the progression advances and the Higher Mind/heart and divine inspiration become your being, your sensitivities to all else changes and the lower mind is crowded out. Then your body begins to be drawn up towards the higher vibration as it entrains towards the stronger vibration. It raises vibration to a higher vibration as it does in healing. As this occurs, new properties—those which you seek now—open and advance, particularly by practice which matures them. These open to the body vessel and come into alignment with the field of the One where all becomes accessible through the process of attention and intention. Yes, it is like fire affecting water, only it is love affecting the body, enfolding it with the love and the light of the One which you are a part of and integrated to."

"Thus it is not a process of letting it all go and to not pay the bills or not do this or that under the Lower Mind. It is not to stop eating and going to work because that instant change creates a void of energy not yet filled with the appropriate Higher energy. This only leads to more distress and worry. But there is a slower constant withdrawal from the demands of the Lower Mind, as filled with the inspiration and compassion of the Higher Mind, the attitude, actions, beliefs, and behaviour shift to take over and fill the void. Letting this happen naturally by letting go creates the new progression of thought, action, belief, passion, harmony, inspiration brought by the Higher Mind."

"Miracles are created when the Higher Mind is able to take its place of command even though this may be a temporary state, But it cannot if the state of being is not aligned in action, belief and passion in the field which is centered in the heart. This alignment reflects your or for example an Energy Healer's truth of being which is the power of the Higher Mind. Such a field allows the energies to entrain, be pure of heart and bold—otherwise it wanes or fades before congealment. This is much like

the wall that limited you from moving to the Co-creation side. More appropriately, the difference is from the fear of your bills being paid to knowing and feeling they are already paid."

So what is this telling us? It was clear to me. It is not as if you have to discover some new part of you that has residency in the sky or in some intangible place because it is already with you. That Higher Mind is the mind of a higher vibration. The best way to illustrate this is with a thermometer which shows an arbitrary scale for vibration from -100 (really strong negative energy) to +100 (really strong positive energy.

The Higher mind does not live in the negative levels any more than love can exist where hatred dominates. Living in both worlds is Polarity. Living on the topside is Unity because you believe everything is connected and if you hurt anything else, you hurt yourself. It is being a total empathic human. It is the same as ice not being able to exist in steam. When you think with the Higher Mind—which you already can do—you think positive—and all your intentions, attentions, perception, and actions are positive.

This is the same place that the Heart lives. So when you are *"dropping into the heart"* you are moving your mind, your attention, and actions into this higher vibratory place. Who is in charge of the thermometer? You? Simply by placing your attention on a thought, creating the intention of doing it by whatever action you make, you choose what part of the thermometer you give life to. How do you drop into the heart? I like the Shaman way of moving the hand from the head, taking the intellect, ego, lower mind or whatever it is that can live at the bottom part of the thermometer to the heart, to symbolically place it in the heart and to believe you did it.

Before I move on, I would like to present some special communications on this topic of going inside into the heart.

How to go inside to reach outside

"A crystal charge has a field that is a special Divine field synergetic with the Higher Self, Christ Consciousness or the Zero Point Field of the Heart. They are all very much One. But this charge is different than the crystal's special signature we spoke of before. Crystals are a divine expression and radiate this special field like they are a congealed angel. In a deep state of meditation or extreme silence, this state is one where there are no thoughts from you—they come from outside, through the field. It is a low state like in your terms mid Theta which is a fringe area not reached by most meditative practices."

"It is not difficult but you must eliminate the noise of your mind and intellect completely. As you begin, place your crystal in front or beside you to simply be aware of its presence. If you are bothered by mind noise and buzz, close your eyes and take your intellect with your hand and simply see you dropping it into your heart, then begin by focused attention on your breathing—deep into your heart. Slowly eliminate all but the presence of the crystal. It may take you 5-10 minutes to do this and as your silence gets empty with practice, you will be able to trigger this faster, like a switch."

"As you drop into this state, you will see the crystal's field and it may even glow like an angel. It is merging its charge with your heart's. This is a divine field and someone will begin to communicate with you. You will know it is not your intellect because it may be a name or a thought, or something that is not known by you. Someone will introduce themselves and begin to communicate, or begin answering questions that have been perplexing you—without you asking. You will sense this as the heart is entraining with the crystal field. This field of charge is one of perfection that is designed to dissolve discord and doubt. It is not a state that is achieved instantly and focused attention on nothing eventually will open up to everything. Your crystal's energy charge will help you attain this faster."

"Now understand that you are able to do this without crystals but this is a faster, more concentrated way of opening up the fields. You do not want to analyze or push this process—simply leave it and feel the energy charge of the crystal—without question or motive. The most difficult part is to eliminate your thoughts and your daily noise. As you get better and the field grows stronger, you will be able to communicate with those that come forward. It will be a soft peaceful interchange. Soon the crystal may even give you a form, like an angel, or a being as seen in your third eye. Soon enough, you will be able to call upon those you wish to communicate with."

"If this is not working for you or you are not able to distinguish between us, we want you to work at this until you can. As you have learned, once you believe and know that we are here and are here to be of service to you, you are in a position to listen to us so we can guide you and answer your questions."

"As we have just repeated, you need to drop deep into your heart and learn to shut out other information that

may be coming in or being processed by your intellect. It is silence you need and focusing on your breathing is an easy way—after you place your intellect on the shelf somewhere. As you drop into yourself, ask us questions that you do not know the answer to. Speak with us, then do nothing except listen. There will come a point if you practice, when suddenly you will realize that it is not you thinking, it is us speaking. That is when your awareness begins to shift and the discrimination of your thoughts and our communications becomes clearer and clearer. Practice this twice a day."

Take your time of peace each day
Drop in to hear what heart will say
But if you cannot hear it clear
Daily fuss is in the way my Dear

RULES | COVENANTS

**A rule is for others to keep you bound
So your true self can't be found
A covenant is a promise only by you
To knowingly follow what you know is true**

To suddenly, cold turkey, let go of everything you know and live the disconnected world full time like Eckhart Tolle is not much of an option for most of us. It seems that a Near Death Experience can make that instant change but this is pretty dramatic. Then there is the issue of giving the think control over to a Higher Divine Mind. Certainly all those amazing abilities that come with giving your Heart, the Divine Command center control are very tantalizing but how do you do this on a planned, proactive basis? We would all love to be inspired and filled with bliss, but where do you start?

I have learned that it all starts with you making an effort. It means to simply open to new information and beliefs by placing attention on them and pulling these into your virtual awareness. Before the universe opens to you, you have to open to the universe. Why? Because the old self and its mind with the ego creates limits of belief and that is the brick wall closing off the universe. It's the other mind of the Divine that is on the other side of the wall. If you can't open to that possibility then it can't come forward to become anything real.

Before you can truly unconditionally love anything else you need to learn to love yourself. Why? Because you are interconnected with everything else and you are on the material structure side of the brick wall. Loving yourself opens the portal to all.

It starts with creating a certain mindset that takes you out of the limits and boxes. In other words, let go of what you know as all of the science rules, and open your mind to a new set of non-science covenants. A covenant, in its most general sense, is a solemn promise to engage in or refrain from a specified action. It is something that **you follow knowingly** under your command because **you** say it is so. This is not like a rule that **you follow blindly** because **someone else** says so irrespective of whether you believe it or not.

The covenants of mind

A belief is formed when you repeat a thought. By following a set of covenants, you make a promise to yourself to engage in certain actions that become entrenched as your beliefs. We all try this as a New Year's resolution but it seldom works. I have found that the 21 day program works for me. That is, if I follow my promises for 21 days, the belief entrenches itself into a continuing habit. On the other hand, if habits are followed for 21 days, a belief is formed that keeps the promises going. These covenants are your own—yours to define, build and believe. Here are mine that deal with the mind.

The Law of One *We are all part of the One and there is no separation from God which is Total Consciousness. Our actions affect every single creature and All That Is throughout the universe.*

The Law of Life *The basis for life is freedom, the result of life is expansion, and the purpose of life is joy as expressed through our perception of experience.*

The Law of Karma *There is a spiritual working out for all things over lifetimes. Thoughts, words, images, emotions, and actions are all energies that we give life and purpose to so as to seek out an energy mate and come back to us in the exact measure in which they were given out. As you give, so shall you receive.*

The Law of Manifestation *Like energy attracts like energy. My thoughts, visions, words, emotions, and deeds create living energies with purpose. They abide by cosmic law to find mates thereby attracting like energies to them as I am the creator of such life. Such energy I give purpose and strength thus drawing material things, people, and experiences into my physical life. I am the power that creates everything in my life.*

The Law of Unconditional Love *Unconditional love is a state of acceptance and non-attachment with all that is and has been which forms no conditions or emotional strings. When you choose Divine love in this way you set yourself and others free, expanding through grace.*

The Law of Intention *The moment I place attention upon that which comes to my mind I am able to create purpose and life to that energy. Intention and action are choices that I make to express myself as to how that energy will manifest into experience.*

The Law of Grace *Unconditional love, forgiveness, and compassion offer grace, which dissolves karma and accrues blessings. It is our purpose to grow and expand the One through us with grace. Grace is the heart.*

The Law of Responsibility *When I take responsibility for my thoughts, visions, words, feelings, and actions* *through my mind, I take mastery of my life. I am able to respond through simple choice to shine my light and love on all that comes to my attention. In so doing all I experience is there so as to grow and improve All That Is.*

The Law of Vibration *All that exists is vibrating energy traveling in circular patterns, unique and with purpose. All energy exists in a wave or perceived solid state. The power of Divine Love is able to interchange these states.*

The pillars of action

Such laws are simple yet difficult to embed. To abide by these I must embed some simple rules into my mind and eventually they will become my belief system that encodes my reality. My code, or laws of behavior require I be aware of who I really am, and live by these simple Laws. Then I build a life based on the pillars of action which are: Give love without conditions; Convert negative to positive; Perceive only for the higher good; Harmonize with all that exists; Be grateful for perfection; Live life in the now; Take total responsibility; Know you are Divinity and deserving.

Now, I would like to present you with my pillars of action that I follow in mind, body and spirit to make it my code of conduct. These are habits that I have imbedded into my life and belief. It is your beliefs that will create the life that you want, and you will find that as you follow these, your life will change as your subconscious becomes re-programmed into a new reality.

First, learn to give love without condition. Give it freely with no strings, expectations, or conditions attached. If you truly understand and believe we are interconnected as one, then these actions are easy because you are affecting yourself.

Next, always train yourself to convert negative to positive. Be aware that everything that exists is in a form of vibrating energy that like you, has a purpose and an intelligence.

Next, perceive only for the higher good. There is no lower good and it is there to simply provide you with a contrast for what you do or do not want. Do not waste time thinking about what you do not want.

Next, harmonize with all that exists. You are all interconnected and by harmonizing yourself, you also harmonize all that exists.

Then, you must always be grateful for your perfection. You are all wondrous beings that have joy and abundance as you choose to manifest around you. Thank yourself and the Universe for providing it so.

Live life in the NOW. As the past and the future have residency only in your minds as perceptions. What is real is now.

There is a shortcut. If you live in your Lower Self then all of these actions are needed to change your attention and intent on a proactive basis. However, If you let go of your Lower Self—put it in the back seat of the car—and let the Higher Mind steer the way, all of the above, and the covenants of the mind are automatic. Here is the short cut.

Be the Oneness of the Higher Divine Mind. Place attention on the Oneness of your Higher Divine Mind— One with the Mind and Consciousness of the One Creator that is of One Mind—Love. Your Higher Divine Mind does not know or recognize what is not love. It seeks only to shine its light and love upon that which is not. That is what you, your Lower Self will move to when you are one with the Higher Mind. The Higher Divine Mind seeks its expression through the heart and then the body, its sensory systems, converting the light to physical 3D experience and hence expression. When you yourself are of Oneness, there is not a moment that comes to you or passes through you that is not a place to shine that love. Oneness means that all is One, all interconnected as one being, all influencing and affecting the other, without exception. Oneness means to feel all else and to see or sense discord, pain, darkness of all that is brought to your attention. For you to shine your light upon it—in love, without conditions, given freely, with forgiveness from the heart regardless of whatever it was that created it. It is to open your heart to what was and is, to allow light to shine on whatever will be to feel the joy of it. Do this in every moment in every day and you will not need to regiment the Lower Self.

The covenants of the body

Your Higher Self expresses itself through a body. The body is used to sense the experiences and the mind records it as a perception and a belief. It would make sense to create some habits that help this vessel work as best it can. What is most significant is that this body is made up of a lower and higher form. And the higher form is not able to express itself in lower vibration. It means that the extraordinary abilities that lie dormant continue to lie dormant until the lower body can sense and express these. The lower body cannot rise if it is contaminated and fed with low vibration energies. Here are some ways you support higher vibration from the Lower Self. I set up a 21 day Body Code to train myself into a new behavior"

Love your body. It is your sacred temple and it is unique. Remember, it is an extension of purity and responds best to positive energies such as love, compassion and peace. It has capabilities and abilities that you are not aware of so treat it as a very precious thing. Remember also that you have to love yourself and your body first before anybody else loves it. Understand that the way you feel about it is directly affecting or infecting its incredible capabilities. It is your choice.

Decontaminate your body. You have spent most of your life contaminating it with bad fuel and stress. You may want to go to a Naturopath or Dietician and find out what your food sensitivities are. If you are overweight or unhealthy, you will probably find that the stuff you like best is the worst for you. That is your ego running the show. Get your body to tell you how it feels, not your ego. What's the difference? The body may thank you for a new eating plan and it all goes to giving the body a chance to get into a better state so it can perform what it was designed to perform. It was designed to heal itself but if your machinery is not functioning well because of a lack of proper physical and spiritual food, it becomes dysfunctional, lowers its vibration and becomes susceptible to dis-ease.

Exercise your body. The body is designed to give you mobility. It is your mind that decides what type of mobility to engage in to maintain best performance. If the ego has much to say about this in later years, your mobility and muscle performance may be compromised. The muscles and particularly the main pump—the heart—simply need exercise to function well. If that engine is not attended to then you know the result. Even if it is a walk in the park 2-3 times a week, the body will thank you for it. Your body is designed to perform as an incredible machine, but it needs to be worked to work well. It will quickly atrophy its functionality if you don't.

Water your body. Seventy percent of you is water. Your brain is even higher in water content. Part of effective subtle energy management must include providing the body with the proper amount of uncontaminated water it was designed to use. A regular amount of water helps to flush the junk out of the body and the organs have less of a tendency to get overloaded and let toxins accumulate. A high majority of people do not take in anywhere near enough to help flush, so of course, many little bad guys like heavy metals and toxins like to build up a strong team to inhibit function.

Ventilate your body. The blood needs oxygen to work well and feed the rest of the system. If it does not receive sufficient oxygen, it cannot transfer air and food into the rest of the system and itself becomes dysfunctional. Deep pranic breathing and aerobic activity helps get more of this fuel into the blood so it can do what it was designed to do, namely make the body work. From best to good is skipping, running, bikes, aerobics, or walking. Take your choice of cure but DO IT. Your blood will thank you for it. You will digest food better and get more oxygen. Even when you are stressed, deep breathing will calm you.

Nourish your body with proper food. This is where you need to start thinking seriously about that hard fuel that the body needs. The ego likes to conduct the orchestra here but you know it would set up a diet of chocolate bars, ice cream and fries for you if you let it. Most don't let it get away with this kind of tune but it always likes to try another craving on you. Don't listen. Your body may have been vibrating to the ego's tune too long and it cannot even tell you what it needs. The statement "you are what you eat" is highly appropriate. Eat junk food and you will rapidly prepare your body for the junk pile. Look to high vibration foods on your plan.

Calm your body. The most important activities to engage in to calm it are Meditation and Mother Nature. Take your time to create clarity and peace. Get out and be one with Mother Nature. Don't get old, get outdoors! The key word here is **REVERENCE**. Use your senses to see, feel, smell, hear, and wonder at Nature. Nature is one of the greatest dividend payers on the planet. Go out and learn to hug a tree. Make it a habit to get into Nature and merge with it — and leave your cell phone behind! Make a ritual of this little sanctuary with Nature. Really feel it and understand the grand beauty of it all. Get a dog! Dogs are trained stress reducers and nature lovers.

My intentions and invocations

I was told that I am a multidimensional being of light. Now whether you believe that of yourself is of course your own choice. But this notion led me to a "fast track" method of changing and doing. This came about because I had a deluge of things that were going through my mind with regards to the four laws of Attraction, Manifestation, Co-Creation and Materialization. It seemed to require a lot of meditation, being still and repeating my hearts desires so as to create the strong energy that would come back to me. In one of the sessions, I was told that this was only causing a lot of extra "work" and there was an easier way if I believed I was indeed a multidimensional being of light.

Of course this was very interesting. What they said was that I, once I had placed on paper a clear description of my heart's desire with its clear outcome, I should choose a word, a mantra, and a symbol to represent this. It is similar to taking any word and looking up a dictionary meaning of it. It has meaning and it also invokes feeling and emotion. Think of the word IRS! A symbol is also used the same way to instantly invoke meaning. It is the same way the right brain works best. The process is to create your own dictionary of words and symbols that have special meaning, triggered instantly by thought, word or image.

By the process of reading these desires that are simple, clear and with purpose of end solution, for three days, you embed these into your conscious and subconscious. By doing this and energizing these with the emotion of completion, you give life to clear, strong vibrational energy with clear purpose. Your heart's desire. Of course remember that your heart will NOT desire something that is harmful or not of the light. Otherwise you fall back to non-divine attraction and manifestation, but if it is speed and balancing and positive desire you want then get the right buddy to help—the Divine One!

Thus, by reading and association, the mind which is already multidimensional right brain super processor can do these things while you are doing other things. And it can continue to vitalize the energy like a multi-tasking computer or image processor.

So I set up my Invocations. When you do this you are appealing to a higher power to invoke your desires. Here's an example:

For creating miracles: *"Being an Interdimensional light being using a physical body seeking perfection, I am now deep in my heart and do call upon Sananda, Mother Mary, Archangel Michael, Archangel Gabriel and St Germain to come forward and assist me in my efforts to heal myself and others who I may be able to assist. I ask you all to place attention upon that area which I am placing my attention on and by my action to heal through focus, intent and faith. I state the word **Done**, either through healing energy through my hands, or healing energies directed by you, that such will be done by us all to bring that area of dysfunction back to its state of perfection. I am grateful for your assistance and by way of stating in thought or word the word **Miracles** three times, **Miracles, Miracles, Miracles**, or by the image of the **Divine Mind**, so declare that my focus and intent together with the joy pouring forth in my heart* *and emotional body do all instantly and unconditionally co-create a miracle of healing. I am grateful for your assistance, love you all and continue to enfold the faith that so it be done."*

So read this out loud, and as you state the word three times, see the symbol in your mind, then sit there several moments charging your heart and emotional body with the feeling that results from the completion of the invocation. Do this for three or more days to imbed it in your subconscious—and your belief.

Then when you have your quiet moment of peace, meditation or whatever and **drop into the heart**, state the word and see the symbol, charge it with a quiet moment of bliss and do the next invocation. If you want to do this every day and simply go through the thoughts and enjoy the completion, that's fine too but go to the heart and let go of everything else. Place the faith and trust in your buddy the divine heart. Surrender to the fact that you have not a clue how this works, all you believe is that it does and there is no turkey on this planet that can convince you otherwise.

Sound crazy? Well, if it does you have not let go of the belief that anything is possible. To find your true self you have to go out of your mind!

Here are some other examples.

Helping Ascension: *"I am deep in my heart and call upon Archangel Michael to place within me, my heart and my complete being the Sacred Fire Love that it will blaze within me to enfold me and my being with infinite Love and Wisdom. I command Archangel Michael to make this fire so strong within me that it purifies and cleanses all that I Am. At the same time I command my Higher Self and Sananda to place within me and my heart the Christ Consciousness and the love of Christ so* *that it remains forever in my heart and guides me in my mortal life, radiating love and sacred energy. I ask also that 100 Seraphin Angels descend onto me and expand my brain and my nervous system so that it and all of my cells can receive the maximum amount of light possible, and that this light as requested from God fire up every electron in my being to become active, perfection and One. I by word of **Ascension s***tated three times,* ***Ascension, Ascension, Ascension****, do assign this upon statement or thought, or associate this intent with the* ***Divine Mind*** *symbol. I love you all and thank you dearly. And so it is."*

And another:

For Abundance: *"I as a co-creator and Intergalactic cosmic Being of Light am now deep in my heart and do call upon my powers to manifest and co-create with God an infinite and continuous abundance, wealth and health. I command into materialization that energy that delivers to me an infinite supply of money that I may enjoy and share the joy with others to make a better and more peaceful love filled life in harmony with all that is. To this end, I command to deliver the initial amount of 2 million dollars and a wonderful home sanctuary of a 2 acre nature reserve with a beautiful home beside the sea so that I may feel the wonder and the joy of living peacefully in harmony with Gaia and Mother Nature. By stating the word* ***Abundance*** *three times* ***Abundance, Abundance, Abundance*** *or by association with the* ***Divine Mind*** *as my symbol, and feeling my emotional body surge with joy, I do instantly create the reinforced intent and focus of my emotional body to feel the reverence and the joy of its completion. I thank you for the assistance and love you. So it shall be."*

And another:

For Changing Your Imperfections: *"I now know I am 100% responsible for that which is in my life and that it is a reflection of an imperfection in me that I alone have created. I am sorry for this. Please forgive me for creating this dysfunction and these issues knowingly or unknowingly. Being deep in my heart I also call upon Sananda, Mother Mary, Archangel Michael, Archangel Gabriel and St Germain and my special Angels to come forward and assist me in my efforts to cleanse all these imperfections and the perceptions that I may have unknowingly created that are not harmony, love and perfection. I love You, I love the Divinity in me, and I love all that is with a deepness from my heart with the joy pouring forth in my heart and emotional body do all instantly and unconditionally ask that any dysfunction or discord be cleared and brought back to a state of perfection. Thank You. By stating in words or thought the words **I Love You** three times, **I Love You, I Love You, I love You**, or by the image of the Divine Mind, I so declare that my focus and intent together invoke these actions and intents. I am grateful for your assistance, love you all and continue to enfold the faith that so it be done."*

This is for opening the chakras:

For Opening Chakras: *"Being a Multidimensional Being of Light, and Co-creator using a physical body seeking perfection, I am now deep in my heart and do now bring my lower mind and intellect into my heart. My Higher Divine Mind is now in command of my being and body. As I breathe deeply in and out I make a connection to the God Source of the One and the Divine Power through the top chakra and therefore open all chakras to the flow of the love and light into my heart. As I place attention to the connection of the Heart and its crystal to the Mother Crystal of Gaia I feel the nourishment flowing into my heart, then radiating out into every cell in my *body and being. As I become present only to myself, I am now sensing my Higher Body."*

*"As I place attention to the red base root chakra, I feel the **material connection** to Gaia and the flow of wholeness and unity into it, opening like a red flower my connection to the material world."*

*"As I place attention to the orange sacral chakra I feel an awareness of the **reverence of the whole** and the unity of all life. I feel my compassion rise as it opens like an orange flower."*

"As I move my attention to my yellow solar plexus chakra, I feel my intuitive gut reactions open like a yellow flower and grow into peace where the true action and intentions are known to me from the heart."

"As I move attention to my green heart chakra, I feel and see the energy field stronger and stronger, radiant and love filled for all that exists. I feel a change increase inside as well as the range of influence, also expanding like a green opening flower to pick up other fields that influence it and expanding my healing abilities."

"As I move attention to the blue throat chakra I open more to communications to all that is and become totally telepathic, sensing other thoughts from all things by my attention to them. As it opens like a blue flower, I sense communications with other beings and all things."

"As I move attention to the indigo third eye chakra, I open to visions and seeing of all things, to see what is new to my higher senses, to open to the vision and sensing of future and energy as in remote sensing, and the sensing of congealing energy of others so as to read its state of attraction and manifestation. I open this like an indigo flower to see other dimensions and beings and

am able to receive visions of that which attention is placed upon regardless of past present or future."

"As I move attention to the violet crown chakra my divine channel opens to all information and the light. As it opens like a violet flower, I feel the connection with all that is and was ever created and know all about me, my lives, and the universe."

"As I move my attention to the top white chakra at the top of my head, I am connected to the light and the universe—the God Source. I open my portal to interdimensionality feeling the lightness of my body. Here like a white opening flower, I open to new powers opening abilities to change and create matter and my hologram by my will."

"As I now breathe softly and deeply, each in breath bringing in energy, each out radiating it into my complete being and through my chakras, I see clearly my total chakra body as a blazing rainbow of color and open flowers, their connections spinning strongly and fully opened. I now will all my chakras to open to their fullest powers and remain in that fullest capacity. It is my will to, upon stating in words or thought the word **Chakra** *three times,* **Chakra, Chakra, Chakra** *or by holding the image of the* **Chakra** *within my Higher Mind, I so declare that my focus and intent together invoke these actions and intents and that they be so done."*

And a short cut for getting connected:

Getting Connected: *"Being a Multidimensional Being of Light, and Co-creator using a physical body seeking perfection, I am now deep in my heart and do now bring my lower mind and intellect into my heart. My Higher Divine Mind is now in command of my being and body. As I breathe deeply in and out I make connections to the*

God Source of the One and the Divine Power through the top chakra and therefore open all upper chakras. I draw love and light into my heart."

"As I now connect my lower root chakra deep into Gaia, I draw her nourishment into my heart and open all bottom chakras. As I now breathe in love and nourishment into my heart, I breathe these out into every cell in my body and being. I now connect my Heart crystal to the Mother Crystal of Gaia as I now connect my Head crystal given to me by Sananda to the Master Crystal of the Intergalactic Council. As I do this, my crystalline Higher body opens and my Higher Mind and Body are now opened to their fullest abilities and are One."

*"I now bring my crystals close to my heart to assist me in my service and amplifying all energies of the heart. It is my will and intent to, upon stating in words or thought the words **I am connected** three times, **I am connected, I am connected, I am connected** or by holding the image of the **Divine White Lotus** within my Higher Mind, I so declare that I immediately and instantly invoke all these intents and actions. And so it is done."*

After you have read these for several days and invoked them, you as a multidimensional being, can further activate them within a few minutes of dropping into your heart. Say the word, see the symbol, feel the bliss of completion for 10 seconds or as long as you want, and go to the next. It triggers the action of reinforcing the energy.

Understand that the purpose here is only for example. Make these clear in purpose and intent, Divine Love based and know beforehand what emotions of bliss they exude from your heart.

Setting the scene (preparation)

I have learned to pull out what appears to be the common denominator in this process of Letting Go. I have learned that what is the important thing about this is not so much the process or steps but what those steps represent. When you begin this adventure, it is like making a plan and taking a certain mindset and intent to action it. When you do this, it is because you believe in it and you know there is benefit in it. By launching simple steps, you create the mindset that impacts your belief, opening it up. From here as the days pass, you create what works best for you. Here is what you are awakening:

Belief that a new process, routine, or procedure has benefit to you;

Surrender to the guidance and command of the Higher Divine Mind and the Heart;

Action of Will by the placement of <u>Attention</u> on some-thing, and the <u>Intention</u> to do some-thing;

Choice of Medium of Action within the Divine Heart where no limits exist and the lower mind/ego/intellect do not interfere;

Awareness of Your Higher and Lower Self knowing that your Lower Self is the physical Lower Body and the intellect/ego as the Lower Mind. Knowing the Higher Self is the etheric energy body and the Higher Mind is the Divine—heart of higher vibration consciousness.

I want to make a side note about crystals. Crystals are symbiotic beings that work with human consciousness and the Heart as they are congealed Divine energy. They can amplify energy, store it and transmit it using the conscious mind as the transmitter and receiver station.

These are your Divine buddies and can assist you if you believe it to be so. If you do, pick two—or let them pick you.

Going inside (being present to the heart)

In a quiet, comfortable seated position, close your eyes and relax, then:

1. Be present to yourself: Breathe slowly deep in to a count of 4 and deep out to a count of 4 into your lower body 3-5 times until you are aware of only the breathing;
2. Become present to the Heart: In your mind, place attention on your Lower Mind (intellect) and state in word with the action of your hand to place them into your heart: "I place my intellect and lower mind into my heart.";
3. Will your Higher Mind to take command: "My Higher Mind and Heart are now in command.";
4. Connect to the God Source: In thought, "I open my Crown Chakra to the Source of the One to draw Love and Light into my Heart.";
5. Connect to the Source of Nourishment: In thought, "I connect my Root Chakra deep into Gaia as to draw the nourishment and love from Gaia to my Heart.";
6. Connect your Crystal: Bring your personal physical crystal to your heart and in thought: "I connect my crystal to my heart as they are One.";
7. Feel the Flow: Breathe slow and deep bringing light through the top chakra into the heart and nourishment from the bottom into the heart. Feel how the in radiates stronger and Feel how every out breath now fills your being and cells with love and light. In thought: "I now open my Higher Body and its chakras to their fullest abilities.";
8. Surrender: Take five minutes to do this so you are now truly interconnected, present to the heart, flowing smoothly, and the Higher Mind and Body are

in command (Higher Mind and Heart are in control of the Higher Body—your etheric energy system);
9. <u>Attention and Intention</u>: Now you are ready to do whatever you place attention onto as you are in the 5D etheric Divine world of Higher Selves.

This process can be set up as an invocation where assigning a mantra can activate it instantly. State as follows: "By my will and intent I assign a mantra of "I am connected" to this process, which upon repeating it three times stated in word or thought will activate it."

In closing, I would consider this chapter as the nucleus of this book. It brings very simple practices into your personal jurisdiction. It, upon your acceptance, cannot lead you astray and it forms the foundation for a new life. Once you have found your Higher Mind and your Heart, things happen. And it leads to mastery of the manifestation of new energies, those you control so the guy in the back seat can really enjoy life.

So where do you want to drive today?
The Higher Mind at the wheel did say
I trust you have my heart in mind
Said the Lower Self from the seat behind

Before you know what within is about
It appears that you must learn without
For the knowing that found in you inside
Is carefully hidden by you outside

The chore is to take action so bold
Create new habits to break the old
But body, spirit and mind must align
Otherwise you may waste your time

PRACTICE | REALITY

**Repeat a thought and it will form
A belief and even physical reform
But physical practice can also make
A belief that can be hard to break**

I decided that I had to create new habits to break old habits. After all, I had programmed me for many years and cold turkey on this paradigm shift was a bit hard to take. You may be different. In my own evolution of this, it all began to unfold when I completed and implemented the Body Mind, Spirit Code that came out in the Managing Subtle Human Energy book. As part of that implementation, many new things that I would never have imagined came forward. One was because of the immense energies I created that went out to seek answers to my miracles quest. Many people, new experiences, and abilities began to open in support of an energetic response. Opening up telepathic communications; like channeling was one of these, as I have already mentioned. What this led to was focused on going to Vibration Boot Camp so to speak, to open new abilities.

It all comes down to how do you let go of what you know and the habits you created. It's not simple. The covenants and invocations were a start as it created the new space. I had to have a lot of coaching. The most revealing came as a set of communications that were first designed to open the mind—create a mindset—by simple awareness and attention to opening the new sensory systems. Many psychics and healers and clairvoyants have these but I can tell you I did not. This was the first stage to let go of that which I knew, place new information into the mind—or retrieve what it knew—and make the transition from imagination to realization. Let me start with the communications which were as astonishingly simple as they were profound in their practical implications.

Opening up the telepathic communications

"We would like you to inform others to open communications to preferred Ascended Masters, Archangels or Angels. You have become aware of one or more of us out here and we would like those that have not yet learned to listen to us to learn as you have. Each needs to open a channel to decipher communications from us. Each may have a preferred way like using crystals or whatever suits them. We can review that here."

"The crystal charge has a field that it has as a special Divine field synergetic with the Higher Self, the Christ Consciousness or the Zero Field of the Heart. They are all very much One. But this charge is different than the crystal's special signature. Crystals are a Divine expression and radiate this special field as they are like a congealed angel. In a deep state of meditation or extreme silence, this Zero state is one where there are no thoughts from you. They come from you through the Zero field. The state of communication with this field is a low energy activity one like in your terms mid Theta meditation. It is not difficult but you must eliminate the noise of your mind and intellect completely."

"As you begin, place your crystal in front or beside you to simply be aware of its presence. If you are bothered by mind noise and buzz, close your eyes and take your intellect with your hand and simply see yourself dropping

it into your heart, then begin by focused attention on your breathing—deep into your heart. Slowly eliminate all but the presence of the crystal. It may take you 5-10 minutes to do this and as your silence gets empty with practice, you will be able to trigger this faster, like a switch."

"As you drop into this state, you may see or imagine the crystal's field and it may even glow like an angel. It is merging its charge with your heart's field. This is a Divine field and someone will begin to communicate with you. You will know it is not your intellect because it may be a name or a thought, or something that is not known by you. Someone will introduce themselves and begin to communicate, or begin answering questions that have been perplexing you. You will sense this as the heart is entraining with the crystal field. This field of charge is one of perfection that is designed to dissolve discord and doubt. It is not a state that is achieved instantly and focused attention on nothing eventually will open up to everything. Your crystal's energy charge will help you attain this faster."

"Now understand that you are able to do this without crystals but this is a faster, more concentrated way of opening up the fields. You do not want to analyze or push this process—simply leave it and feel the energy charge of the crystal—without question or expectation. The most difficult part is to eliminate your thoughts and your daily noise. As you get better and the field grows stronger, you will be able to communicate with those that come forward. It will be a soft peaceful interchange. Soon the crystal may even give you a form, like an angel, or a being as seen in your third eye. Soon enough, you will be able to call upon those you wish to communicate with. This is a repeat of the crystal information we gave you."

"If this is not working for you or you are not able to distinguish between us, we want you to work at this until you can. As you have learned, once you believe and know that we are here and are here to be of service to you, you are in a position to listen to us so we can guide you and answer your questions."

"As we have just repeated, you need to drop deep into your heart and learn to shut out other information that may be coming in or being processed by your intellect. It is silence you need and focusing on your breathing is an easy way—to place your intellect on the shelf somewhere. As you drop into yourself, ask us questions that you do not know the answer to. Speak with us, then do nothing except listen. There will come a point if you practice, when suddenly you will realize that it is not you thinking, it is us speaking even though this is the same as your own thoughts. That is when your awareness begins to shift and the discrimination of your thoughts and our communications becomes clearer and clearer. Practice this twice a day."

"We know many of you may be very left brainish, that you will doubt communications as being real. It is useful to work in pairs so that if both of you communicate to the same source, on the same question, it should be simple to confirm each other's answers. This is what you have done with Beverly. You have asked us a specific question one day, then you asked Beverly to ask us what we told you about that topic. She has then confirmed what we told you and that has given you much confidence in your communication."

"All of humanity are receiving information and guidance from the higher realms whether each is aware of it or not. What we prefer is that you all become much more aware of this and open up the channel for more direct communications. But begin with a belief that this is the way it is."

"As you continue to open communications and as you go deeper, it gets to be automatic. You will begin to simply know things and know that these communications are not of your own intellect. They are of your mind yes, but they are part of the higher mind that is connected to all that is. As this becomes stronger, you will not be doubtful about your knowing. And that which you need to know will be brought forward by your asking."

"You see it is the way of things. That you must ask to know what you desire to learn about. It is true that when you are with heart, that your heart will let you know when things are not right but it is not so when you want to learn. What we will tell you is never of negative or conflictive energies because we do not exist there. So when there may be some doubt as to where the information is coming from, check with the heart and see. Think of the expression 'I know in my heart'. It cannot fail you and those ascended beings all work through your heart."

"This is the way to guidance and knowing and as you practice this, it will become stronger and stronger. After a time, you will not even need to be in the quiet space of meditation as you will be connected continuously, communicating with us through the heart. This is always the case already but you, as with many, have not been able to tell the difference. That is why you need to learn to drop into your heart and listen for our messages. Before long you will be able to distinguish different telepathic frequencies or voices."

Opening the chakras

"As you are now at your sanctuary as you call it, it is time for you to complete your book and to review that which we have brought to you of letting go. It will be your special time to bring your attention from out to in,

then in to out and practice your progression of evolution. Take your time and learn to unlearn that which has limited you. Let the senses of your soul open now and blossom as you know its purpose and presence. This is your time and place to re-remember."

"Be patient with this and set your attentions to the bliss, the simpleness of your surroundings and learn the truth of the beauty surrounding you. Yes, we will coach you now in your quiet meditations and attention inwards. As the stronger this becomes, the more it will open to you."

"Open now at a special time of day the crown chakra— and above through your Divine Self and feel the no thing of it. Go to this place twice daily as your habit. It is your inner sanctuary and you will begin to understand that which is outside is so inside and that which is so within is without. As the world of in and out begin to congeal you will know when the shift to the next plateau will begin and open to your Divine Self. This is your time, your in and out, make it so by not making it so, meaning surrender to its process instead of trying to make it happen."

"You are learning to drop out so you can drop in to your parallel reality. These are individually yours as part of your whole. As you learn to walk both worlds you will keep the benefits of both—eventually to experience both together in any moment. Learn to at first drop out as in your meditation but make this a serious attentive experience to drop attention. Yes, it is a paradox. We suggest you set a little ritual to do this by becoming present into the heart."

"Then begin to connect through the top chakra above your head and the Earth chakra below your feet to ground yourself. Let the energy flow. You may want to flow discord downwards into the Earth to be cleansed. Then become present to parts of your body from the

bottom to the top, simply place attention here and sense what is there that is different. Then follow your energy system and feel and sense the parts that come to you in a mindless state. It can be a sensation, buzz, warmth, let it flow and be and let your awareness be taken to those places."

"Then leave it all and drop out bringing your Divine self into your heart. Sit with it and be as it wishes to be. Yes, you have dropped out. Do this twice daily—at night before sleep and a separate session at day. We suggest that you accelerate your progress by deeper concentration on your body and energy systems. You have been distracted and a clear place of peace and comfort is needed for you to place attention in."

"We also suggest you start sensing Gaia's energy into you at first connection. She provides the nourishment so feel this work upwards through each energy center. We will start with 7 centers that provide skills that begin to open. These are yours and always have been. No one has given them to you any more than the ability to eat sleep or love. They are yours to develop as you choose. The two that are below you and above you (9 in total) are your connections to above and below."

"At the first base root chakra you will find the material connection to Gaia and the flow of wholeness into it. Here a warmth or some feeling of unity will prevail. This is your material connection to everything on this planet. Simply feel the connection to all that is and you are part of it."

"At the next level of the sacral, you will begin to feel an awareness of the reverence of the whole and the unity of all life. Your compassion will rise here."

"As you rise to the next, the solar plexus, you will feel the intuitive gut reactions grow as the action and

intentions being monitored as appropriate. These will grow stronger to guide you."

"At the heart level, the field will be sensed as stronger and stronger, radiant and love filled for all that exists. You will begin to feel a change increase inside to sense a larger influence, also learning to pick up other fields. This is your healing center."

"At the throat level, you will open more to communications and become more telepathic, sensing other thoughts from all things by your attention to them. This will become stronger as you pick up and transmit. Your communications with other beings also increases in intensity."

"At the 3rd eye level, attention to visions and seeing that which was not seen (at will) accelerates. This vision involves (future) and current seeing, remote sensing. You will sense the congealing energy of others to read its state of attraction and manifestation. It is used to see other dimensions and beings as well."

"At the crown level, the divine channel opens to information and the light which is all. This is where you will have connection with all that is and was ever created and know about you, your lives, and the universe. This will grow stronger as your communications channel opens to know and understand all. We are working on this now."

"At the top of your head you are connected to the light and the universe—the God Source. It is your portal to interdimensionality as the lightness of your body changes and you begin to launch your other stronger abilities to change and create matter and your hologram by your will. The control of matter and opening to the new laws of the metaphysical science come under your command. This will bring the following skills to you;

levitation, bi-location, telepathy will be improved, invisibility, teleportation, and materialization."

"So it is a progression that will evolve through your practice. As we said, hold onto your hat, because the top of your head is the portal."

Developing the healing

"Yes, today we will speak of your healing. It is as you have done with your mantras. We suggest you set up a special one for healing. This requires that you relax and breathe deeply to bring attention to peace and the heart. There are many ways of healing and you will find a way that will suit you that will feel right. But they are all based upon a fundamental mindset of belief, faith in yourself and the heart. Bring your lower mind and intellect into your heart. Bring to you your Higher Divine Mind knowing it is now in command of your being and body."

"Bring in your connections first to the God Source of the One through the top chakra and open all chakras to the flow of the love and light into your heart. This is your Divine power."

"Bring a connection to Gaia up through your chakras into your heart opening them to the flow of the Mother's nourishment."

"Bring your assistance into your presence and attention with Sananda, Mother Mary and Archangel Michael to see them descend to you, ready to serve, clean and replace that which is required."

"Bring in your responsibility with the statements that you love the area of attention, are sorry for any disease, dysfunction or discord that you have created unknowingly or knowingly through your perceptions and

that you wish to be forgiven and that divinity has permission to bring it back to its state of perfection."

"State that you are grateful for all of the assistance in creating a more joyful, love filled world."

"Set your will. Will this all to be so, stating that it is your will—to be in your heart, to surrender to the Divine Mind, to connect above and below, to have Divine assistance to serve and to replace that which you are placing attention on."

"With your words of a mantra and a special symbol you will that the association, action and attention be immediately instated and invoked upon statement in mind or words and the symbol. At the end you can feel the completion and state - And so it is Done."

"Do this out loud for three days or more to register this into your process of being."

"To do the healing, begin with the vision of the heart and the mantra three times keeping attention on it. Feel this in your heart as it opens connections and see the descending of the divine assistance."

"To heal a part of you like your knee, once ready and settled and present in your heart, place your hands on either side of the area of dysfunction. Breathe deeply to keep focus on the flow and strength of energy. Breathe deeply in to draw the light and love of higher vibration from the God Source and Gaia into your heart."

"Breathe out slowly seeing the energy move out from your heart to your hands and into the area. Do not place attention on the dysfunction or issue but on the energy flow to see it clearly and feel the bliss of the solution of perfection. You can visualize and feel the joy of it not existing as you send this love and light into the cells and

the DNA to revitalize them to reflect the way they were meant to be. Hold this for some time until you sense it complete—at least 5 minutes or until you sense you are done for now. This will bring the lower vibrations into the higher. You will simply know the Higher Divine Self and Mind and your assistance are clearing and replacing discord, disease, dis-ease, dysfunction and disharmony with love and light. How is not significant."

"To heal yourself as a whole, project yourself (Higher Mind and etheric being) outside of your body to see it standing there. Do your mantras, see the divine assistance descend, then begin your breath in and out projecting this energy to the whole, enfolding it with the love and light from your heart."

"If you wish, you may imagine and use your etheric hands to place these on two areas of the body—each being drawn to these locations. You will let the Higher Divine Mind sense this. In your mind connect these two as you breathe in and out. Feel the connections and see yourself renewed, joyful and bliss as there is nothing that is not of the light and love. State that It is so Done."

"This will be the same process you will use on others at a distance. You may not know what has been changed except that something has been changed and is different. See the image of the person doing a happy dance, or laughing with happiness and tears in their eyes. You will also feel the compassion of it as bliss."

"Doing this will lead you to miracles as you are awakening your Higher Divine Mind and your true nature as a creator into action and this will lead to instant transformation of matter. This is where the pure Divine Love has the greatest power."

How to create a CrystalNet

"We would like you to begin experimenting with a group of individuals and crystals. Each will hold their own crystal and a central crystal will sit in the center between you. This requires you going deep and energizing the crystals by connecting to the heart, breathing deep to a count of 4 or 5 in and out then seeing the energy flow out of your heart into your arms and hands to the crystal. Do this for 5-10 minutes to make the charge strong as every out breath increases the charge. Each of you should do this, moving the energy into the crystal. It is best to have someone in the group that is already psychic and can see and sense energy as the verification will quickly impact your belief."

"Once this is done, each will point their crystal at the center one so it can focus its energy through its apex into the center. Each of you then places attention of the process of projection, seeing the beam being absorbed into the center crystal. This has now created a small CrystalNet like your Internet."

"Now each of you can send thoughts of an event or experience as a short few lines of something that was wonderful. It can even be an image. As you do, send it with a tag on it, like one of the participant's names, moving your attention to that person. This is like an entry signature accessible by that name or frequency signature. By forming the words, seeing, and feeling it gives more strength to the clarity and power of the packet. This is something you can play with and experiment with. And yes, it is simply practice!"

"Each can do this and it can be for all or one. It can be imagined to move along the beam like a cell phone connection and asked to be stored. The purpose of the central crystal is to amplify the power. It charges if you

ask it to especially with healing energies that need to be stronger, held until it is accessed."

"So the same can be done with healing energies through the heart with intent labeled for the recipient. You can call this T-mail if you like and you can work together to amplify energies—like in manifesting or remote healing before the central crystal transmits it on its way to the recipient's heart. The recipient can either access it themselves through your CrystalNet or you can all beam the concentrated energy to them directly."

"The power resides in the amplification, storage and ending/receiving of Divine energy. You can learn to form these networks and beam pictures, books, thoughts, feelings. And you can learn to eventually tie in to all that is, into the deep data banks of the Universe."

Practicing invisibility and bi-location

"Now we speak of a practice that is a progression of invisibility-bi-location-teleportation as one leads to the other as the body lightens."

"To begin, you will start in a quiet meditation state which centers you on your Higher Divine Mind and the lightness of your Heart. They will first absorb the lower mind to take command. This process will lead to the phase shifting of your holographic body into a synchronous plane with your etheric self or your energy body that surrounds your physical body thus being invisible to lower human senses. We will call this the Higher and Lower Bodies."

"Thus you do not disappear as much as begin shifting into higher vibrational plane like a cloaking so it cannot be seen by the normal senses of others—unless they are of higher vibration and can do the same."

"Once under the command of the Divine Higher Mind and Heart, focus your attention on your feet or hand. In your Higher Divine Mind ask it to now with the help of the Divine Heart shift its form into the form of your Higher Body."

"See it begin to fade its outlines and you may feel a tingle, warmth or buzz as the heart responds. Try to close your eyes to a point where the image of the hand or foot is fuzzy. Keep attention on this seeing it being shifted into a dimension with your Higher Body. Simply will this to be so. They are still one but the phase shift creates a cloak which is not seen by the usual range of brain senses that create the hologram of reality."

"Focus for several minutes on the will you are giving intent to. Open to this idea to your parts and players. Yes, you can use your crystal to help as this is natural to a crystal. You can practice this on your crystal, asking it to phase shift as well."

"The exercise is simply one of awakening to the belief, the self and your body. But you now understand that this process has much to do with the level of vibration in the physical body—your Lower Body. The more light that is within, the higher is the vibration and the easier it is to shift upon command. Heavy lower minds and bodies will not achieve this as it is not within their range of senses and the properties which are not yet active and remain dormant. It is like learning anything else—the ability to swim is in you but if you do not train yourself to do so it will not be. This exercise will institute the awakening and intent and attention and it will grow stronger with practice. But like swimming, you must believe you can do this."

"As it progresses, you will shift from a part of you to the whole of you to be cloaked in a higher plane. To bi-locate, you would simply walk to another location and

will yourself to reappear or shift out of the cloak. To teleport, you would simply project yourself to another location or dimension and reappear. You are all part of the One anyway so it becomes a simple matter of choosing an attention target and willing it to be so."

"Teleporting, however, is a much greater topic as there are many other ways. But these nevertheless rely on learning the lightness of the body to prevail, and the connection with the Higher Divine Mind, and your Light Body. It is the Divine Love that is the true power. Yes, it is all simple but as you are learning, the rising of vibration to allow these to happen even though they are all natural abilities that all process as Co-creators, is not. The rising of vibration is a process of life itself, as reflected in the way you live life, behave, and believe. Be patient and attentive to the One and the Oneness of all and practice this with faith. You are attempting to unlearn what has taken you lifetimes to learn. Tomorrow we will speak of telepathy."

Practicing telepathic abilities

"Yes, we speak of telepathy. Initially you will use your mantras to establish a process and use your symbol which will instantly trigger the actions and intents. Then as you awaken to your abilities, they become as automatic as speaking or writing. This is your goal over the next months."

"If you remember when you experimented with your divining rods, when you stated: 'I shift my attention to ...' the rods would swing in alignment with the thought energy field as a channel or beam from your mind. It was like a channel that opens to a specific frequency as attuned to the signature of that which is being focused on. It is the same here."

"As you state this and it is your intent to hear the words or thoughts that are spoken or directed at you, you create the intent to pick these up in the open channel. Similarly if you state the same as to sending a word or thought, the other may pick it up as something that pops into their consciousness."

"Important it is to be in a state of mind and in the heart so that the mind accepts this—as you simply accept the truth of communication with us. Your mind must be free of clutter and noise from the lower mind and ego. With all of this that you learn, that state is of silence, belief, and acceptance to the truth, placing your Higher Divine Mind in command of your thinking and it is an integral part of the heart and the Higher Body. They all synchronize into the same medium of love of the One to act like a switch that turns the power on for the information to flow."

"Start simple with a friend—a word repeated several times by the other when the channel is opened and you are in silence. Ask the other to make the statement of intent and focus and try this. In your state of peace and silence, outside of all else—which is inside—do this until it works using simple words."

"It is simple and it is directed at first to open then become more automatic to open to other thoughts."

"You may then become tuned to other's thoughts by the simple action of placing attention on them (creating the connection) and letting information flow (statement of intent). Yes, it is that simple and as you know now, your abilities are stronger as vibration rises. Never forget this as lower vibrations cannot facilitate this any more than darkness can exist where there is light. This makes the channels stronger and with focus as well. Such is impossible with those who are of lower vibration and with a busy lower mind clouded with ego and analysis. It

is the heart and the Higher Divine Mind that speak and listen softly with love and compassion for all."

Practicing teleportation

"We begin a simple individualized practice of teleportation to get your minds and bodies attuned to the process and awaken you. This is a simple process which of course becomes instant by action, intent and attention to the location chosen. It is a process of lightening and projection."

"Your components are higher and lower minds and bodies and the heart. Sitting peacefully, place the lower mind into the heart so it does not interfere with you and belief."

"Next, eyes closed, relaxed, choose a location close by as your end point, and a position you will move to. See yourself being filled into the heart with a beam of light through the top of your head and see yourself lift to project yourself into the desired place and position. Look around (with eyes still closed) and note what you see around you in the new position. Hold any images and feelings. This is a first level. Now after a few minutes of looking around, bring yourself back. Yes, this is all in your imagination."

"In the next stage sit again the same way and choose your place and position. Bring your awareness to the Higher Mind and Body."

"Bring a beam of light down into your heart filling it with love and light to overflow into your complete body. You will feel a lightness, tingle, warmth as the body fills with light and love from the Source."

"Now with attention on your Light (Higher) Body, feel its presence and let it begin to rotate clockwise around your

Lower Body. It will cause a sensation of joy as it rotates creating a vortex and it will feel light, you want to lift up like a helium balloon. Rotate faster and then project both bodies to the new location. The Higher Mind simply places the Higher Body there holding the Lower one which has been temporarily merged into one Light Body. This is invisible to most others which cannot do this. This is simply what you are so you are temporarily moving to your natural multidimensional state of a Being of Light."

"Look around to see and feel things around you. As you stop rotating you congeal back to your form."

"This will take time and later you will project yourself to some place that you have not been before and recollect the feeling and images of what is there."

"Eventually you will have a high enough vibration and a lightness that the two bodies are more aligned and synchronous—enough to allow a direct teleportation by simple intent and attention to the new location. Do not be discouraged by this as taking its time and work on the first two levels. The purpose is to awaken and make your mind aware of the process so the rest will unfold."

Practicing crystal telepathy

"As you hold your new crystal, you are being telepathic with it. Yes, you are 'out of your mind' speaking with it. It is as in a conversation, transcending language just as we have none except what is chosen as resident in your awareness."

"The crystal that you are working to make glow is the one we want you to begin more remote sessions with as if it was being held by you. This is building to the awareness and ability to simply place attention on any object to begin communications as you do now. You are

learning that the attention and intent is all that is required with your ability to listen."

"Crystals are a special reflection of the beauty of the God Source. They are perfection that has materialized as an ascended state of nature and perfection. Their makeup is already an expression of the Divine and all that exists in the state of no thing which is every thing."

"In effect you are the same and can link to it by will, anywhere, anytime making this truth to your Lower Mind and body as it ascends into the higher states. You see it is already all there."

"Crystals are wondrous symbiotic partners wanting to serve—especially humans and have immense powers individually and collectively like you, but require the relationship with humans to be directed. Although they cannot do negative things they can be misdirected for negative purposes by humans who are misguided."

"We ask you to begin practice with your other crystal to pick up telepathic thoughts. Place it in a different location (have another person do this) unknown to you and see if you can sense its surroundings. First make sure this relationship is set up close by like when you practice making it glow with energy from your heart."

"This will lead to remote sensing by simple choice of an object or something representing say a picture of what you choose to be telepathic with."

"Once the connection is made, the communications between you is automatic, has no effect by distance, and places your Higher Mind and 3rd eye there, with your power to sense into that location as if you were there."

"We wish you to do this and practice. At first you may not feel anything is happening but remember what you

had as doubts about us. Keep faith and act on simple practice of attention, intent and listening peaceably and quietly within the heart."

Practicing remote sensing

"We spoke of teleportation which is to send yourself to other locations. Yes, we are pleased to see you forming your network of crystalnet as it will become our focus later. It is good to bring your crystalnet into your sessions. We speak of a process to develop and sense in other locations away from you now. Here your Mind takes your attention in and about other locations where it can feel, sense, see, as with your usual abilities. The difference being is that the Higher Mind is so doing with Higher abilities."

"This is like you asking in your healing to bring attention to a place or thing or organ in the body to see, feel, or sense something that is different or to pick up dysfunction, discord or unneeded energies. You are moving your attention to a location in your mind to determine what is there, describe it for the purpose of qualifying and quantifying it—even communicating with it once it is identified. Yes, it is because everything has a purpose and is living energy."

"Similarly we wish you to practice this on your own body to go to locations, areas and do the same. We suggest you learn to do a scan or a sweep of yourself—as this will lead to sweeping others—to sense, feel or see energies and properties."

"You can work on others the same way as you begin to form a picture and a perception of the point of difference or you begin to do the same about any object or environment your attention moves you—simply by the intent of so stating or thinking in your mind. Project yourself to different locations, places, times, dimensions,

realities, and future as you do in regression and as in the healing you just did. Yes, these are different techniques. You will create your own basket of personal processes and techniques when your confidence and comfort level grow."

"Then do the same in a day dream state as well. This process will affect your healing and teleporting process as well. As this develops you will begin to open your senses. For example you will move your attention to a new location and think about smelling, feeling, and hearing. What is happening here is your sensory system heightens and expands its ranges as your Higher Mind taps into the physical AND etheric bodies."

"You will begin to move attention to others and sense, see, and feel the energies as they open to you. This will expand as you simply place attention on them, in them, and around them with the intent of sensing energies."

Practicing materialization

"On your practice, we speak of materialization which will evolve as your vibrations rise and body lightens. This is indeed a higher vibration ability that lies dormant in all. Again, it is attention and intention and love as the substance of power that allows an image to congeal into a material representation of an object in a hologram."

"This means that the Divine Mind must be the total agent of the image of some object that is simply created in your mind's eye. It will be a clear image so you need much practice here. At the point at which your Higher Divine Mind and the Heart—the congealer—create that image, it is projected onto a place of choice by intent. At the same time the image in the mind is projected to the God Source of the One to be reflected back like a mirror as a beam of divine light to the same place of choice— yes it is like converging laser beams of light."

"As these two actions converge upon the place of choice from you and the Divine beam from the source, they form a holographic duplicate representation of the object that is to be replicated or materialized. Yes, from a wave form to an atomic form as the electrons arrange themselves into the image which is your higher consciousness choosing a new possibility from the no thing."

"No, you do not concern yourself as to how the chemistry, atomic structure and so on occurs. It is all under natural cosmic law that such an arrangement is created. These laws understand how this is done and your Divine consciousness abides by these so they all understand what this is made up of. They know how to congeal this into the physical expression of the holographic image. Then it can be interpreted as such by your and other sensory systems of your brains—your sensory receiving stations."

"What we want you to get used to is this concept as you will begin with simple things all in your mind. As you sit quietly one with your heart and Source, knowing your higher mind is totally you, you form the image and project it. Then from your image, project it to the source to reflect back onto the same spot to see it materialize."

"You still need to enhance your image and vibrations which you are doing so rapidly now. So do this in your mind and then there will be a surprise one day when your vibrations have increased. Suddenly you will open your eyes and it will be there as you imagined."

"You will develop and expand over time as you begin to understand the laws of nature—and the Divine laws of Cosmic creation. At first you will not see material results of your efforts as your belief system adjusts and you surrender command to the Higher Mind. Here you are

adjusting to the belief that the infinite possibilities of your mind are awakening. We only want you to begin this process to instil it as an eventual automatic process of a Creator."

Practicing psychokinetics

"We will speak of psychic abilities especially those of moving and transposing material objects. This will allow you to place attention on an object—your crystal you are now attempting to glow for example—and move it by changing its properties. We suggest you link to your crystalnet, from the heart and Higher Divine Mind for assistance. Surround the crystal with a ball of light infused from you, then attach properties of lightness, no gravity of something else attached to it like a balloon, all in your mind."

"Visualize a rotation of the ball around the crystal and see it lift and move upwards. This will be with your eyes closed and in your mind. Direct this to another location or bring it to you. This will also evolve slowly for you and at some point be stronger and stronger. This is also the way to transforming properties."

"Yes, now you are seeing the power of the Higher Mind. All you must do is vibrate higher from the heart."

Practicing clair-abilities

A clairvoyant is someone who has the power of clairvoyance. Clair meaning CLEAR and Voyant and Voir meaning TO SEE. So a **clairvoyant** is said to be able to see clearly. What is really meant by the term clairvoyant is the ability for a psychic to see what normally can't be seen, or to see the future or to see the spirits of people who have passed over. A **Clairvoyant Reader** is a person able to see spirit or see the future and conduct a reading. **Clairaudience** is the psychic ability to hear things that are inaudible, meaning a psychic hears beyond the natural sense of hearing. He or she may 'hear clearly', and perceive sounds or words from spirits, guides, or angels or simply hear into your future in some mystical way. **Clairsentience** refers to a psychic's ability to pick up sensations and relate messages from those sensations. **Clairaliance** is to be able to smell aromas beyond the physical levels. **Clairtangency** is sometimes used to describe a psychic's ability to touch beyond the physical. **Clairempathy** is to be able to feel emotions from beyond natural realms. **Clairgustance** refers to taste. Some psychics will be able to pick up certain tastes while conducting a reading.

"Yes, we will speak of clair...abilities. These are the abilities that are part of your higher body and mind. Like your lower body has its range of sensing abilities and systems that are processed by the physical brain, the higher body has the same abilities processed by the higher mind and the heart which is also like a brain. It links the two as the etheric and physical hearts are one linking the body and the Divine."

"It is as if you came to a new location and began to see, smell, hear, taste, and feel new things. But as you know these are operating within a narrow band of vibration and there is a much higher range used by the Higher Mind. These reside within the higher vibrational sea of Divine love."

"What this means is that as you project yourself, or your higher mind into a new location, or situation, you begin to use your higher Clair...abilities. So you are now applying your senses into the invisible world rather than the physical visible world."

"Now you see energies, new light, other beings, feel new energies of light, love and sense vibrations. Now you hear new sounds telepathically and pick them up from all

things and beings. Now you know information about these energies as you tap into the fields. Now you interconnect as you are One to feel compassion. Now your higher chakra system awakens to new ranges and experiences."

"What is happening is your Higher Self opens and your higher abilities expand and you begin to see ghosts, entities, talk to spirits, read the future and read energies that are being congealed awaiting manifestation. These are the psychic abilities that come with connection to all and being one with the field of all that exists."

"There are many of these that open and many that are not understandable to you yet. It evolves as vibrations increase—yes we know you are aware of this now!"

"To practice this is simple—continue your expansion of your chakras as you are doing with your friends and Shea-Ri, your special Angel. But we want you to begin to do this in an awakened state as well, after you have done your session with eyes closed."

"Sit there and be one with a scene in nature. Look at everything slowly and carefully after you will yourself to be in your heart, and have your Divine Mind in total command of your awareness and your higher body to open its sensory systems. Activate this with reverence and love."

"As you look around, begin to see things through the Higher Self (mind and body) and these invisible new senses to see what have not yet been seen before— auras on trees, energies playing, new sounds, new things, beings talking. Pick up feelings and simply scan to see what is new—different than your usual senses. As this develops, you project into a new place and do the same. You will begin to form a new vision of everything around you as your oneness with all opens and you

interconnect. You will begin to see everything in a different light—the light of higher vibration and higher energies."

"As this opens to the world of one and the world of now, it forms to you as past and future congealed into now. It is all there as the same source of all. As your compassion, love and reverence open, you begin to see all energies, including discord, disharmony, disease, disease and dysfunction as energies that you read and feel—as a divine empathic being that can be corrected by you."

"Take your time daily to do this as it is not meditation with closed eyes, but attention to the greatness and the power of life itself."

Practicing energy sensing

"It is the ability to sense energies of others. There are many energies that living things create and by opening your own to the Higher Self you will begin to quantify and qualify these energies."

"Because the heart is the conduit and the command center or the brain so to speak you will feel empathically the pain or pleasure of the energies. It is important to understand that balance is needed so you do not bring dark energies to yourself. You must then balance these by compassion to heal but with an nonattachment to it as you feel and sense it."

"Energies are created by others which are blocks or dark energies as a result of experience, contract, others who have more powers or wish control or harm, creating discord and disharmony. These may be from other times, current or future, in that they may be already there with purpose and life or they may be congealing in intent having been given life and purpose to manifest.

These can be knowing or unknowing through the attraction and manifestation process. They can become stronger approaching the time of manifestation."

"These are energies that you can tune into and begin to draw the information attached to them that surround their purpose. Once this is detected you may even begin to communicate with it to help it or the one it is attached to (like in your healing practice)."

"These can reflect past current or future and your new senses will begin to pick this up. To some extent, you do this now as you feel others presence or mood intuitively. Psychics read the future this way. This may be manifesting in the now as a contract whose time has come (future) or energy of fear, pain or disease created in the past."

"Your practice is to learn to tune in to this through your higher abilities and help to cleanse that which is not right or discord should it be necessary. Remember that these may have a purpose for others and you are not to absorb but balance. You will sense purpose and the link to the others higher mind will reveal whether it is necessary to cleanse. You will sense this and it will build in you to feel the interconnection of you with others and all."

"Practice by paying more attention to this as you use your expanded senses being practiced now. Subdue the lower and dominate with Higher."

Practicing intuition

"Yes, intuition is powerful and you have already intuited what you must do in your healing. Intuition is the knowing of what is right or wrong—knowing what is the right intent and action. This is stronger now when the Higher Mind and Body think through the heart. When

you are at a thought, an action, a response, idea or something that is about to draw your lower self into action, stop and allow higher access to this. By stopping the lower mind you are not giving thoughts an acknowledgement they are there. You are not creating an urge or desire that gives the energy life to attract an experience."

"You will know or feel its energy essence as to whether it is in harmony with your heart's vibrational essence at the point of attention. The gut feeling or shiver in the spine, or the tightness in the throat, or the tightness in the chest are the nagging of 'not right' reactions of the heart vibration through the chakras. They are calling for balance. You will begin to sense this in yourself and others as you learn to let go of the lower mind (ego) and the body. As you tune to others actions or statements (at first) you will sense the same by the densities of energy around them, tapping into the fabric of information."

"You practice this by keeping the Divine Higher Mind present always as a habit. Simply say it so. Ask it questions of what you should do, or act upon. But be cautious of automatic negative impulses or responses without pausing and consulting. Learn to feel the energetic body discord as your sensing system unfolds and your heart and upper mind take their command positions."

"Do this by sitting quietly and asking things and test this. Ask about things you know are right or wrong and pay attention to the emotions, body sensations, feelings that arise."

Practicing levitation

"Yes, you have levitation on your mind. This is a special form of bilocation and it involves filling your body from

the heart with a lightness and creating rotation to change the gravity field which holds physical bodies in place. There will be two stages. One is to do this in a mind state using your imagination with your eyes closed, the other being in an eyes-open normal state."

*"We are giving you a Golden Angel of Light. Yes you will name her and the name Auran comes forth. (*Note: Just ask for one.) *She will help you with this. First you will close your eyes and sit quietly placing your Higher Self (Mind and Body) into the Divine presence of your heart. Your heart energy field which you call a donut or torus will now draw energy from the light through the top 9th Interdimensional chakra as you draw each breath of the Light and Love. You will begin to feel lighter first in your heart and then it permeates the physical body. Auran will enfold you as you bring this intent forward and as you begin to rotate your higher body in a counter clockwise rotation within this field, a vacuum forms below you as gravity is not there."*

"You will begin to feel a floating sensation and enter the zero point field with the assistance of Auran and the Higher Mind, you can lift upwards."

"This is your first stage. When you do this physically, you will be focussed the same way and set a mantra to activate the process. As you concentrate attention and trigger the intention of the light and rotation, together with your angel Auran's help, you will provide light to fill and lift you. Of course the level of vibration is important as it is lightness so this must be practiced."

"As with all of these higher abilities, the process you use is not as important as the light, vibration, attention and intention as commanded by the Higher Mind and the Divine Heart. You will reach a stage where it is simply a process of thought, attention, intention and action as

you do now in your physical lower state. There is no real difference except your belief."

"At this point you will see the commonality of all this and the need to move your thinking and belief system into the invisible world—the lightness of your Higher Self with the Divine Heart and higher vibration that will come with practice and attention."

Launch a practice program

"We are excited to see your CrystalNet grow cosmically and see your invocations to evolve the expansion of it. It grows now to us and intergallactically. We would now agree you are ready to practice what we have told you. For the next week you should develop your program which we will help you with."

Invocations*: "First you may review or create your invocations to assist you to create the same attention, intent and action rapidly. This helps to define the same energy each time. You will add one for opening your chakras. These new ones you will read by word out loud for three days to imbed them. Then your invocations should be read once per week to enforce their energies."*

Morning Session*: "Your morning session will then contain as you do now but link to us and the CrystalNet first. Go to the heart and command the Higher Self to be in command, then state your invocations. We will then, after that communicate as now."*

Day Session: *"During the day, you will set your time and place to do your full chakra program as we have given you to open to your Higher abilities. Once this is done you will place attention on the chosen practices for a week. Each of the practices we have given you can best be instilled this way by choosing a few each week. Go through these quietly and in your heart, with the*

Higher Self in command. You will first set these into your mind and being. This will be expanded later and do not concern yourself about results—only attention to process and intent with the Higher Self and Heart."

Evening Session: *"Here we wish you to practice with your CrystalNet, each time holding a different crystal to your heart. Yes, you can hold these in thought as well if they are not physically available. In this session you will communicate with the one crystal being held even though they are all interconnected as One. During this you will be sending love and light energy from the Source to heart and into the CrystalNet. Then sit in silence for a few minutes to feel the flow of energies. At the end you may wish to communicate with the crystal and take notes on your messages."*

Before Sleep: *"Before sleep, we suggest you connect to us, Gaia and the CrystalNet to ask for downloading of questions and things that perplex you. You will invoke your visits and travel here and with your new senses opened ask that all be remembered upon awakening. We shall see what that brings."*

Here is the bottom line. Level of vibration, strength of belief, and purity of Divine Love dictate progress.

It's your lightness that is the key
But first the Heart must be set free
Higher Minds just wait around
If ego and density bog them down

BEFORE | AFTER

**It is time I said to my Higher Self
To take higher thoughts from off the shelf
and walk these thoughts as if real
To transpose to reality what I feel**

At some point in these writings, one has to face up to the real bottom line. That is: "So Mister Ed, how did you do with regards to what you preach is your truth? Did you activate and develop these higher vibration abilities of ascension? Did you attract, manifest, co-create and materialize things? Did you learn how to at will do all these metaphysical things that make science a joke?"

I started awakening at the end of the century. I had to get out of the boardroom of corporate life to do it. Hopefully it will not take you 50 years to figure this out. The big switch was when I began to dissolve anger towards the commercial and spiritual conspiracy, blaming it and other things for my ups and downs in life. The result was a series of books called ***The Book of Secrets*** that revealed how and why the deceptions had been placed upon us, and what to do about it. There were two solutions presented here that unveiled how commercial and spiritual sovereignty could be regained to use the system to your own advantage once you realized who you really are. The basis was that in the case of the spiritual deception, I had been convinced that I was beholding to religions and those who told me I was **not One** with the Divine; I was separate and polarity was the rule. I was taught I had no Divine powers and that metaphysics was nonsense. I was taught it was these top guys—popes and gurus and bishops and those religious name tags were the ones who knew truth and were the gatekeepers to Heaven. Us other guys were born in sin and we had to gain salvation. They alone could lead the way—you may have to make a tiny contribution or some such thing. What a crock! Well, the truth was that me and the Divine—the Creator—**are One**! There is no separation! And by the union of the two, new rules of spirituality opened to a new sovereign.

The commercial deception was the opposite. My training was that all commerce and the laws, the statues, and the workings of these were imposed on me as One. In fact there was another me that I was trained to believe was me. That other me was called a Strawman—a dummy corporate entity called a Trust—that I was led to believe was me. They had to do this to have me agree to give up my God-given sovereign rights, unknowingly. The belief that we were One allowed the rules and regulations to be imposed on me because I accepted that corporate entity was me. Well, the truth was that me and the Strawman were separate—not One! And by the separation new rules of commerce opened to a sovereign flesh and blood human.

As the parallel paths along the trail of deception unfolded, the analogy to Martial Arts began to hit home to me. The new abilities and the new rules presented choices of how these are eventually used and deployed. At first, I took Martial Arts because I liked the idea of being able to defend myself and also pound the piss out of those that would try to attack me. But like most martial artists who get to the top of the heap, a transformation more spiritual in essence develops. When they have the confidence and the knowing that they can defend themselves, they find an inner peace where they know there is always a higher power; albeit a tougher black belt. They shift into teaching and training others to learn the same. So I wrote the **Commercial Martial Arts** books to learn the commercial tactics on the private side of sovereignty that was non-conflictive.

What also came out of this series of books had to do with managing energy—mine! What I thought, said, felt and acted on was having a considerable impact on what my life unfolded for me. It was the beginning of the **Awakening** stage and the Law of Attraction.

It was here that things began to shift. Up until this time I had been sleeping, listening to what others told me. It was here that it was time to learn to be a Reiki Master to learn healing, and pay much more attention to the energies I was creating. It was time to raise the awareness of psychic abilities, clairvoyance, intuition, and meditation. *It was time to regain my Spiritual and Commercial Sovereignty*.

As I explored the pathways of sovereignty and how I actually attracted things in my life, I began to sense that like the Martial Arts Masters, I had to master the Art of Energy instead of self defense. It had to shift away from anger, conflict, defense, and hostility to more positive energies. Anyway, all this negative stuff was creating more of it and taking its toll on my health.

It seemed that my energy that I alone created was somehow attracting similar energies to me, manifesting in experiences and situations of the same signatures. This was pretty hard to believe so I began to test this and study it.

The true sense of it all came after several other books came out of me culminating in **Managing Human Subtle Energy–Walking the Thought**. It was where I began to understand how I was attracting things that I was unknowingly manifesting through the Law of Attraction. So I began a program which I called the Mind, Body and Spirit Codes.

Now, if you look at the following chart, scan the stages of evolution, and in particular the abilities that open as the stage increases due to vibration. At first glance these abilities in the **Awakening** may be of interest to you?

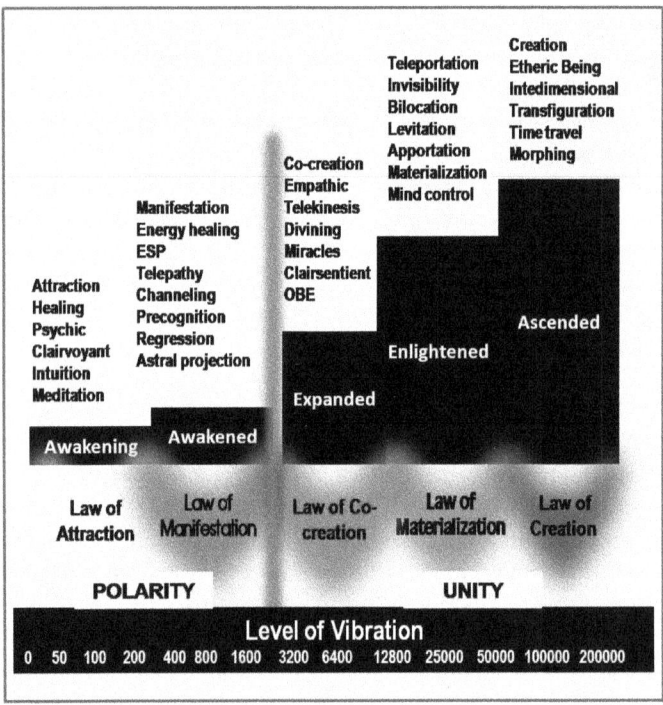

These may seem esoteric and metaphysical but sorry; the Law of Attraction ain't metaphysical! And if you can change your life with respect to wealth and health then perhaps you may want to pay attention to the **Awakened** part?

I had 24 hours in a day like everyone else to create energies. Being financially oriented I set up a human energy fund. Here I took full responsibility for managing four portfolios. I was going to take the management of the fund away from my broker—namely my ego and take responsibility for managing it with my new Consulting Advisor; the Heart. It would guide me on a great growth scheme. The Heart was going to help manage my energies of thoughts, images, words and emotions.

My fund was made of four different portfolios with energy assets. These related to the way I gave life to different energies. The more positive the energy, the higher the value of my investment. The more negative the energy was, the lower it would fall.

I determined that the initial investments in the four portfolios would reflect four types of energy generating activities. The first two portfolios were *reactive* energies. One was a result of my thoughts created from the news, the media, television, papers, what others told me, things that were outside of me. I called this group *media*. I listen, hear, see, read and react, creating energy. Perhaps 60% of my total time in the 24 hours was of this nature.

My purpose was to not react in a negative way. No negative thoughts, no adding of negative emotion, never getting angry or saying things shooting from the ego's lip, or doing things that would not be in alignment with the heart. Yes, it is not an easy task in such a negative world.

I would stop a thought before I gave it life and remember it was there to teach me what I did not want, and focus on it, not the reverse. If I reacted instantly in rage, it was my ego. I would simply stop the thought for three deep breaths, let ego subdue and let the heart take over. Then I would create a new reaction that saw a good reason for the issue, or not react at all; keeping it neutral. I had to remember my objective. It was to invest in a future life of goodness, so the more goodness I could energize; the more I could build up the value of the portfolio and the return on my investment. At some point it would return to me through the Law of Attraction. Positive grows the asset, negative diminishes the value.

The second portfolio I set up also came from outside of me and is part of the reactive. It had to do with events that happened to me that were seemingly not under my control. This was my *events* portfolio like if I had a dreadful accident, or you got involved in a terrible situation. This I figured was about 10% of my energy fund. My immediate ego instinct to clash, react, or do something that I could be sorry for later was the issue. The focus was NOT to do that. Not to create a huge energy action that is negative. Try to see some reason why this occurred to me and read something good out of it. Take a higher perception and see in it a lesson of what I did not want or what was good about it. I knew if this was some terrible thing that that would create anger and vengeance I had a choice. It was my choice to go ballistic but if my portfolio was to build rapidly, this is the place I could make huge strides. I knew many of these could be a result of old karma or negative energy in escrow from the past. My tactic was that it was a terrible problem that put me in fear or hatred, I would leave it alone for three days to get the ego out of it then have time to look at it with the heart in mind.

The next two portfolios were *proactive*—those energies that I myself could create in my own time, purposely and with positive purpose from *inside*. The first was easiest described as *free thinking*. It is the time I would spend letting my mind simply generate thoughts about whatever was on my mind. This I figured was about 20% of the time, or 20% of my energy fund.

This was like when I created a thought about my own personal affairs, like about a feeling of inadequacy, doubt, fear of the future, crisis from the past, not enough money, or feeling sick. Perhaps it was about how great the world was, what I have to appreciate, what is good. My focus here was to add to the positive investment energy in my fund. I would with purpose and intent add my own positive thoughts. Any negative thoughts like it pisses me off, or I hate this, or I feel crappy, would not be allowed to enter my portfolio. I would learn to stop this and convert it. I would not give it any negative life.

The last portfolio had to do with plans. I called it the *plans* portfolio, also from *inside.* I figured I could have 10% of the fund allocated toward this. These energies were for investing in major desires, solutions, passions for me to manifest. Here, rather than being focused on the problems, like not enough money, having to work hard, do this do that to get more money, I would change the focus to the solution. I would feel the energy of completion, add the emotion of enjoyment, be grateful for it being done, and put the positive energy of completion out to the Zero Point Quantum Field to attract the solution. I would place this energy in my fund. This I thought could be a very small part of the fund but it could have an immense effect on the positive energy of joy that could come back into the fund and its future value.

Well, I began to see a dramatic change in my life as the fund grew from positive energies. My objective was learning to generate new positive energy or convert more and more negative energy until there was no room for negative events and experience to enter my day. It was like a business where you take old energy companies that are failing, then put new energy into them to be successful.

I was aware that I could have residual energies in escrow that were looking to materialize—things I had already given life to. Some may be there as lessons or karma that would manifest an experience that needed to be converted. I would celebrate them as a great opportunity to create a big impact in my fund. They would be great opportunities to point a different way.

Well, it was not long before I started to attract a whole different set of people of like mind. And new options began to form. It also led to new books: **You are Fired Said the Heart to the Ego, The Way Back, Xolani and the Magic Shanty** and **Jack and the Great Oak Tree.** You can see from the titles a new world was manifesting rapidly.

The book on **Subtle Energy** left me perplexed about how this subtle energy thing all worked scientifically—since I always had this science niggling. And could this new discovery of managing my energy better translate into managing physical events? Could it be used to manifest healing miracles—particularly on myself and others I knew needed help? So in my proactive part of my portfolio, I began to change the nature of my attention and intent. This brought many new people and experiences, and information into my domain.

And so it started a new quest. After giving life to the energies of intent here, I began to uncover the answers rapidly, resulting in the book: **Miracle, Miracle I Wish to Find Where You Hide Within my Mind**. This was a study of those people who were creating healing miracles around the planet. After all, if miracles were real, why could I not do them? As my quest materialized in new people and values, things took me into that **Awakened** stage on the vibrational scale. I began to channel to Higher Ascended Masters—although I did not understand how or whether this was in fact true. I found it was true as I verified it by other channellers and healers that came into my life. I learned their techniques. I began to open my manifestation abilities and energy healing abilities. I began to heal others, not as a business but simply because they needed it. I got better and better at it. I began to open communication with crystals. I was assisted by Guides and Angels. I began to unfold a new reverence for all that was. I became telepathic with these Guides and Masters, and I began to learn all about astral projections and many other things. I learned regression. And this is when things began to accelerate.

The book left another question about health miracles yet without physical solution. It was time to increase the attention and the intent of my portfolio. Through the new people and information, and the telepathic channeling that was a daily ritual, I wrote the book: **The Way Back** about my own lifetimes that I discovered and opened to me.

But there was still something missing. I still had some health issues and I still wondered what it was that I was supposed to do on this planet? Did me and my soul mate have a destiny that I was not following yet? Well, I will not get into it now but I can tell you it poured out and is still pouring into the book: **Chronicles of an Ascending Planet** which is still being written.

But the miracles, attention and the telepathic communication led to the other side into the **Expanded** stage—and Co-creation. This book is the result. But I had to learn to *Let Go* first.

So what do I do now? Well clearly I had to "go out of my mind" to find my truth. So now I walk around talking to myself, ascended beings, angels, rocks, crystals. I have meetings independent of time in the sky. I think about people and heal them. I take people back to prior lives to heal their energies. I communicate with Higher Selves. I create all sorts of energies that manifest for me. I get answers to questions that I didn't even know the question. Does this sound like I have gone out of my mind? Perhaps! Am I headed for the Loony Bin with a rubber room? I don't think so. There appears to be a big Looney Bin forming as you will see in the next chapter. It's for those that cling to old ways of materialism and do not go out of their mind!

And what about the rest? What about those invocations about finance and health? What has happened? Well, that is a whole new story. All I will say is that it has unfolded so beyond my dreams, I can only shake my head in wonder. That is what the next book is about.

What if I create all I think and feel?
What if it's a movie I believe is real?
And what I believed is what is not?
Would I then change the plot?

MAN | GOD

Am I man or am I God?
It is my knowing that sets the odds
As I am One and One is all
I can command all I call

I am going to leave you with an interesting series of transmissions on Ascension. But first a very old picture.

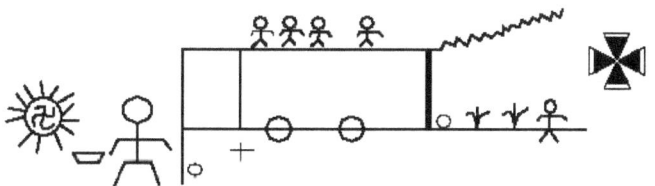

Near Oraibi, Arizona, there is a petroglyph known as Prophecy Rock which symbolizes many Hopi prophecies. Its interpretation is:

The large human figure on the left is the Great Spirit. The bow in his left hand represents his instructions to the Hopi to lay down their weapons. The vertical line to the right of the Great Spirit is a time scale in thousands of years. The point at which the Great Spirit touches the line is the time of his return. The "life path" established by the Great Spirit divides into the lower, narrow path of continuous Life in harmony with nature and the wide upper road of white man's scientific achievements. The bar between the paths, above the cross, is the coming of white men; the Cross is that of Christianity. The circle below the cross represents the continuous Path of Life. The four small human figures on the upper road represent, on one level, the past three worlds and the present; on another level, the figures indicate that some of the Hopi will travel the white man's path, having been seduced by its glamour. The two circles on the lower Path of Life are the "great shaking of the earth" (World Wars One and Two). The swastika in the sun and the Celtic cross represent the two helpers of Pahana, the True White Brother.

The short line that returns to the straight Path of Life is the last chance for people to turn back to nature before the upper road disintegrates and dissipates. The small circle above the Path of Life, after the last chance, is the Great Purification, after which corn will grow in abundance again when the Great Spirit returns and the Path of Life continues forever. The Hopi shield in the lower right corner symbolizes the Earth and the Four-Corners area where the Hopi have been reserved. The arms of the cross also represent the four directions in which they migrated according to the instructions of the Great Spirit. The dots represent the four colors of Hopi corn, and the four racial colors of humanity. After the Great Purification, one path disintegrates into chaos, the other continues forever.

Now, remember the idea of the vibration of the body that was studied by Valerie Hunt in Chapter One? The level of vibration is what is referred to as Ascension. This has many meanings but here it means to ascend higher. In Christianity it means the body of Jesus rising. In the New Age it is the process of raising vibrations. It is to choose the Higher Path (the lower one on the Hopi picture).

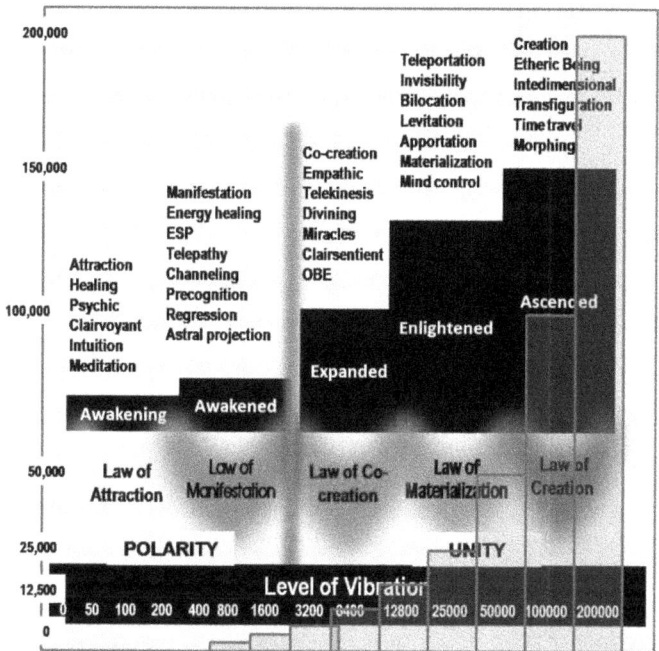

Have a look at our old graph that shows the stages of vibration and the levels measured by Valerie. There is a bar chart plotted overtop showing the frequency of vibration. Its a bit cluttered but what is important to note is that things don't really get going until your vibrations get into that **Expanded** stage. Then hold onto your hat because the speed at which things unfold doubles each time!

With this ancient and new information in mind, I want to present messages that were recently given to me about this Ascension thing. I want to see if you are "out of your mind" yet!

Ascension and YOU

"Let us speak of ascension. You have been placing attention on your ascension and the process of change within you. It is the rising of the spirit and the body, drawing the body of the Lower Self to a higher state of vibration of the Higher Divine Self by entrainment. You can see now how the Higher Divine Mind when in command and maintained in its higher vibratory state of the heart, love and light of the One uplifts the Lower Self towards it lifting its vibration. The Higher Body which contains your chakras and invisible (to you) etheric double works this way. Your Higher Divine Mind, when in command of the self interconnected to the heart and the Source, draw the body into a higher state of vibration."

"As this proceeds, the body begins to show its lightness and begins to change its properties, being filled with the love of the One. Its functions, abilities, and characteristics begin to open and expand—much like you are working on now in your practice. This is why it is important to have the Higher Mind in its proper place first and expand the light and love to make this entrainment stronger, aligned with the Divine Self and the heart. Many already have developed these abilities to some extent by being of the light but these are not the many. These abilities are but a fragment of the whole that is possible."

"You are now approaching a time when these are indeed opening as the body entrains upwards toward the higher state of a love based reality. The stronger this is in your daily actions, attention, and intentions, the faster this process proceeds. Of course this is also happening to all as the process of ascension is not limited to one. But the majority will not know that this is upon them and will be like children who will choose not to follow this. Much like humanity has ignored the abilities and the call of

ascension even though it is written in them to seek out their divine selves."

"By attention and practice, these individuals who choose the path of ascension accelerate the process and reach a point where the workings of the hologram and interdimensionality become one; where abilities, knowledge and the co-creator within unfold rapidly. This is what you are attempting to do as the different dimensions and abilities open to your awareness and attention—by simple intent."

Ascension and GAIA (PLANET EARTH)

"We will speak more of ascension which is of Gaia. Like you, she has a Higher Body and Consciousness of Mind with her own purpose of ascension. You as a living being are symbiotic with her and depend on her for your nourishment as you are all one. She is also higher and lower. Her invisible system of energy which is like your own chakras and light body is of higher energy designed to relate to her cosmic self. She herself is but one of the chakras within a larger being. She and her larger cosmic being as well as that of the Universe are in a special time of ascension. They are drawing their physical living counterparts within the hologram of the Creator to higher realms of energy."

"She is drawing her physical body upwards as are you. The draw is the cosmic vibration of cosmic bodies and vibrations as they move in cycles and orbits towards a special configuration of a special time. There is no choice on this as in your astrology it influences the vibrational setting which affects all consciousness and all things. Although you, as special cosmic beings of creation, have the will to choose alignment with this or ignore it, Gaia does not and hence she will ascend as many of humanity will. This process of ascension is much like your own in

that it evolves into a higher form of lighter body high vibration as the larger beings do as well."

"How this process unfolds is dependant on the symbiotic relationship and the joint consciousness of the creators— you. For if you choose not to move your lower selves into the next vibration, then you remain in the lower form separated as many are now. You will not evolve with the Higher Self—eventually following the path of death and incarnation in the mortal world as has been so. Gaia is dependent on this consciousness as it relates to how her own physical expression will grow as we and it and larger beings in a symbiotic relationship of the One—the God Consciousness. This is the nature of things. It is important to know this so that you as the creators carry this to the rightful ascension process of all that is. This is why many eyes are upon Gaia and how her symbiotic creators unfold the physical ascension."

Your relationship with the planet EARTH

"We continue on ascension as a symbiotic relationship between all of humanity and Gaia. You depend on her for nourishment and the One Source for the spark of the Creator. She also depends on you for your consciousness and the way you live upon her as One in a natural relationship of harmony. This has not been so and much is in discord where Gaia feels and manifests the dysfunctional energies that congeal into her physical expression. As ascension proceeds and Gaia's Higher Self draws upwards her Lower form, her own vibrations rise. It is so because the larger being that she is part of is rising rapidly now. As she rises, so do all living things upon and within her, drawing them into a higher state all living things and energies that rely on her. As this quickens, it opens and awakens in the humanity the DNA and the cellular structure shifting towards the Light. The shift will then quicken towards a place of decision of all beings. Many are now of the knowing of what they must

do and what changes are to come. And many are withdrawing from the old ways of ego and the attraction to the material realm, finding the true strength of the heart, in peace, relationship, and love in their existence. They are accepting graciously the new gifts and increasing the vibration of the One of relationship, of harmony with all matter and things and with all life, being drawn within to the heart, enfolding with new perceptions of the Light and the Love of the One."

"But there is a split in this path and you have written about this as signs reflecting vibration which you call sleeping, awakening, awakened, expanded, ascended that are appropriate. As you have noted, it is a pathway that is aligned with the laws we have spoken of Attraction, Manifestation, Co-creation, Materialization, and Creation. Indeed these reflect an expansion in vibration and to the true abilities of you as a Creator Being of Light and the evolution along the path."

"This path is one which is in a setting within the material hologram of your life, and as the energy of this setting is influenced by Gaia's own vibrations, the influence of other cosmic forces from larger beings containing Gaia, and other cosmic waves pouring the Light upon you and her. This is being felt by all—as all of humanity is on the same path. Some, as you, as conscious co-creators of the God Creator will feel these and sense these more than others. But the path will split at the point where the Law of Co-creation is actioned within. It is the point at which you have stopped awakening and become One with the Divine heart and are indeed expanded. Yes, it is another sign marker on the path."

"The split in the path will require choices and even though the changes in DNA and the Lower Selves are gifts given freely to all, the choice is whether such will be accepted and how the awareness enfolds and unfolds with you. It will evolve at different rates for each and

some will not accept this at all. How these gifts evolve and are utilized, and in what Light they are used is a choice. At the basic levels of awakening and awakened all will have the experience and receive, wonder, ponder and be surprised at these new abilities of healing, manifestation, and psychic abilities. Yet others will block them as incompatible to their beliefs. These will open to the many and many will begin to use these in service to help others, also opening other's awareness."

*"However, the point on the path which is a big decision is to let go of the old and to be One with the Divine part of you, placing the command in the Divine Higher Mind and being truly within the Divine Heart and to truly raise the vibration into the Expanded realm. Yes, a higher path with a sign that says **Let Go—Divine This Way** and the Lower Path that says **Hold On—Ego This Way**! It means letting go of the old energies of the material shift to the Higher Divine Mind and Heart commanding all your gifts, your consciousness, your energies and your eternal life as part of the Creator. This is the path that opens to all possibilities, is dimensionless, and is the path of ascension. It splits from the path of descension and indeed separates between higher and lower paths. The higher path opens to total awareness of cosmic laws and your rightful place to walk all worlds, dimensions and create at will. Such right of will itself has its own evolution as the light and love of the One increases. As your material hologram unfolds its workings, as you have written, the new path begins with the laws of co-creation where miracles occur, and materialization where new possibilities are formed through the mind. This is only your beginning on this path."*

"For those that choose to walk the lower path, the choice to open to the upper path remains but their transition will be different. Many abilities due to higher vibration in the body begin to show and will cause those to ponder and perhaps be frightened of the abilities. Being able to

manifest faster, being more intuitive and telepathic, and to heal others will come into awareness. It may create a rift in their consciousness. But they will remain on the awakened state in terms of their lower bodies, retaining their Lower Minds to be in control and this path, which is not a true path of the Divine Heart. It will continue possibly making their lives difficult as they begin to see the laws of attraction and manifestation at work—faster and faster. As this quickens, the draw will be strong to shift and many, like you will be there to help them realize how to let go and move to the invisible realm of the Divine Mind, the Heart and the One. But those that do not will continue to create the hologram world of material and low vibrational energies. We will speak of this later."

The Higher path

"We now speak of the Higher Path. This as we have said and you have shown as the progression of higher vibration from the awakening to the ascension. The choices and road signs are along the path coming to you as signs of the awakenings in your Lower Self, and in your body, mind, and chakra energy systems. As the Higher Divine Mind takes its command it knows how to progress and at what pace to expand just as your Lower Mind knows what pace or limits to impose to guide you in a physical or learning activity in your regular 3D life. This higher path of learning and physical adjustment is no different except that the Higher Mind guides with the heart from a higher perception through divine inspiration and practice, always being within the higher vibration of the One."

"The signs along the path come to you as your higher body chakra system casts away imbalance and dysfunction by your attention and will to open to their true functions of expanded senses and abilities. These are indeed the ones you are opening in your practice

sessions and are best exemplified by your invocations and practice. Let us start from the main chakras from the bottom."

"Your lower one is the Earth chakra. It is below you, encapsulating you, and connecting your etheric double to the Mother Gaia. It is your grounding, drawing the nourishment of the Mother to you. As it awakens, it firmly connects your being between it and the upper chakra above you which is the connection to the One, the Source, Heaven. It is the heart that balances these two. As the awareness of these opens, the flow between them allows the others to awaken to their full potential."

"At the Root, the awakening brings the knowing that you are part of all that is Gaia and all living things. It is about it all being One. The sense of completion, of wholeness opens here as a reality. At the Sacral level, the wholeness is expanded by the reverence and the wonder of you and the relationship to the whole—to Gaia and what she and all living things are and being all interconnected. The importance of the wondrous relationship expands here."

"At the Solar Plexus level, this connection to all is of the knowing of the will and the action and intent by way of the power of the intuition; how you relate is sensed here as to what is right in the relationship and aligned with the heart. At the Heart level, the emotion, the feelings of love and compassion prevail as being drawn by the nature of a true empathic relationship to all that is you and the One. It is your feeling and healing center, one of knowing and sensing the discord so that it can be cleansed, healed or brought back to a state of perfection—in perfect alignment with the heart and the Source."

"At the Throat level, it is all about communications with all that is. It is the ability to telepathically connect with

all living things and to sense their states of evolution and purpose. At the 3rd Eye it is about seeing all that is and all within it by the attention to it. At the Crown it is about the connection to all that is to the knowing of all that was, is and will be. It is the connection to the God Source of all knowledge and knowing. At the very top is your Heaven chakra, the portal to the Universe; to interdimensionality and the connection to the Father, the source of the spark of life itself."

"These all expand as your Upper Path evolves and the body begins to change, dropping many of your material and physical needs. As the high side of each chakra awakens, the lower side drops away or fades in importance and as your abilities open to those you are practicing now, you begin to co-create in your lower world and you begin to shift your attention to the higher world—as you are finding now in your Interdimensional sessions. These as you see now have no bounds. They are but a tiny part of what is unfolding. As you progress on this path, you learn to walk both worlds. What you originally believed to be imagination and a fabrication is not. Your physical body becomes lighter and of the Light and it is able to drop its many needs like food and air and other things that your etheric double—your Higher Body—does not require. And it will take you into these upper cosmic planes that you begin to experiment with as you do now. You will be able to bring this body with you at will thereby bringing Earth to Heaven."

"At the same time, you as your Higher Mind and Body will bring what you learn and know of Heaven in the upper dimensions to Earth. Yes, all balanced and commanded by the heart—the command center between Heaven and Earth—the Father and Mother. These worlds become interchangeable at will. Along the path are your road signs and markers. You are seeing these markers as your own telepathy, healing, channelling, galactic travel and manifestation skills forming the as above so

below interaction. These are unfolding on you and thus enfold a new life upon you. You are at that stage of the expanded phase of the journey, where the partnership with the Divine and entry to the other side on the High Path is your reality. This path unfolds rapidly now while the lower path continues. We will speak of this path next time."

The Lower path

"The lower path is a choice of any who ignore the calling of ascension. The process which unfolds in them will be the same as others and new surprising abilities will open. These, which have been thought of as metaphysical or esoteric nonsense will develop in all at the cellular DNA levels but may be confused, feared, or ignored. Many may attempt to commercialize or use these for their own dominion or fame. But many will not and when the healing, telepathy, empathy and manifestation begin to rise in all, any advantages or dominion will cease, as will the drive to commercialize for profit. Motivations will be easier read as the intuition and energy reading improve. As the ascension quickens on these, resistance or fear may manifest itself faster as will all thoughts and feelings but others like you will be there to explain this and to assist in the graceful shift of mind to the way of the heart."

"Some may not heed or want to change their ways and they will continue on the Awakening Path bringing upon them dis-ease and discord faster and faster until they recognize the reasons of cosmic laws. It is no different than now and their lives will take a normal traditional path of reincarnation. They will simply be reborn again within the same hologram as now. We do see many changing and many to teach the new truth. As you see, the process of ascension is shifting not only the physical body but the lower minds as the mass consciousness entrain these to a higher plane. Many may withdraw

from the old ways to seek new away from separation and polarity, and conflict and dominion of one soul over the other. The ones who remain on this path will be crowded out and the consciousness of the new will begin to resonate stronger and stronger as the evolution continues. On the upper path, the evolution accelerates creating more and more that will teach and more and more that will raise the mass consciousness vibration faster."

"At any part of the lower path, a choice is always there to partner with the Divine Heart and move to the Light side. As the contrast between the paths will become more obvious and visible, impossible for the establishment to ignore the process will begin to switch as a minority will usually follow the majority. The major change will be that the majority will teach spiritual sovereignty where no one has dominion in the laws of the One. At first, those who stay on the lower path — those that have not reached the vibratory level of the Divine Self and Heart, will leave their bodies as is now. They will be recycled back as the new crystalline essence as are newborns now. There will be a point where only the recycling occurs and no new souls are needed but in any case, the DNA will be fully activated in these, coming into an evolving consciousness of new mass consciousness, knowing the truth and being supported in the new energies, already wired for ascension. This process will begin to shift Gaia and her relationship with humanity. How this unfolds is not written, and what Gaia chooses to leave along this holographic path is up to her and the symbiant consciousness of the living things upon her."

"There is, however, a minority of power lords who are of the dark and cherish dominion over others. We will speak of this next."

Those who choose dominion over others

"There are those that choose dominion and control over others. This is as it is because you choose this path and it is because your DNA is encoded with the lower vibration of the lizard humanoids that was crossed within you long ago. It, being void of Spirit, has provided you with the basic needs of instinctual survival but it is not aligned with the heart. It can be triggered easily in you and the ones responsible for activating this within you are well advanced in the cosmic ways of energy being able to manipulate humanity this way. They are of course void of Spirit by choice as they know that by creating fear of death, pain, loss or discomfort or insecurity, it invokes low vibrational energies of cosmic law to bring more upon you to prevent ascension and awareness that you are more than this low vibration. Knowing also that part of humanity's DNA encoding is to seek a greater power, by manipulating the religions, they attempt to satisfy this draw but also control it to deceive. Yes, that is the way of it."

"They are of the knowing of the working of vibrational energies and the different dimensions of it and how to use this to keep humanity in the lower state. Through time they have been successful in this by taking dominion and control through this process of subduing your spiritual, physical, and commercial sovereignty—as you are well aware of."

"If we speak of these dimensions, they understand how to work in the higher invisible etheric planes of energy within the holograms. For a simple example, you are learning that you are within a physical material plane you call 3D. You are learning that your energies of potential congealment are in a temporary transitional state of 4D. The 5D plane is where your Higher Self also is as it reaches across all dimensions but like your physical body, may not yet be awake. As you can now

understand, the thoughts and energies you create begin in 5D with attention, action and intent, waiting in 4D, ready to manifest in 3D. As above, so below. This is a simple example of course but this is the way you as creators create in the hologram—the level of creation being your level of vibration. The ones who prefer dominion and are heartless know and use this well. Think about your two paths of upper and lower and how you have become aware of this invisible world (to you) of the hologram and how you can "as above so below" transpose and transmute energies. On your Higher path of ascension when the Higher Divine Mind enters its appropriate place to be aligned with the Heart, you enter a new domain because you are indeed all One—all sovereign entities of the whole living with unity and the purpose of the heart—love of the One. You can view this as the 6th dimension where peace, love, compassion of all that is, is the total domain."

"Of course, those who choose to control know they can control without conscience of the heart or spirit by avoiding the heart with exception of their own blood lines. This is their undoing. Thus they can kill, threaten, raise fear and bring conflict without mercy or compassion as dominion becomes their passion. They have also learned that subliminal devices, and many ways of triggering the lizard energies can be used to confuse, change and reshape the transitional energies of 4D and also confuse the purpose of the Higher Self of body and mind at the 5D level. However, at the 6D level this is no longer possible as this is now where the Divine Higher Self exists and it is immune to such things because of its higher vibrational plane that cannot support lower energies. It is the Divine, the heart, the true connection to higher holographic planes of Love."

"As you have seen, this is the plane that you are working within and you yourself are reaching into. Your own awareness and practice and attention has shifted to the

power of the higher plane of the love of the One. You also can change the energy of attention and intent of others Higher Selves who have fallen and are unknowingly acting on the as above, so below to create the situations and experience driven from above. It is here on this upper path that the lower vibrations begin to reprogram themselves in the DNA as it opens to the Divine by transposing the lower energies that are not needed and hence dissolve and atrophy. You have atrophied your true powers the same way."

"Thus there are many who control knowingly and it is so because humanity has let this be so. They are choosing separation and polarity by placing attention on the importance of the 3D world's material gratifications, allowing dominion. Much like the ones who appear heartless and choose dominion, the heart is of local nature with close family members, not with the whole or all others which are in reality all family. Yes, it is the inherent lizard DNA that wants to protect their close bloodline and destroy or subdue others who are perceived as a threat."

"Yes, you may feel that the use of 5D knowledge is unfair but you now realize that you also have an unfair advantage of rising to the 6D level. Think carefully about this. When you enter this consciousness along your upper path, you can help attain the light, and assist in dissolving the energy of dominion of one over others. So who has the advantage? You do. It is a matter of awareness and choice, attention and perspective is it not? That is the way of it and remember that there is no right or wrong in this. It is all part of the hologram and the living energy of Consciousness of the Creator—the One that has a purpose of perfection."

"How these heartless beings who prefer to avoid the heart act is no different than the rest of humanity that choose to be in the heart with their preferred family

members only. That is the big question of ascension destiny and the paths chosen. It is your purpose and your groups purpose to transmute this into the light as being part of the One—the one family of all that is. This is as you are learning now. Your further advantage is that energies they have used for dominion are fading and shifting. Many are awakening themselves as their material world also fades to realize a more fruitful and fulfilling way of Spirit and oneness. So as the consciousness energy of Gaia's ascension shifts, and fills the air of all that exists on her with a higher vibrational essence, it gives you all the advantage to walk where they cannot and to indeed help all equally to see the light, does it not?"

The cosmic influences

"It is more on ascension we will speak of but on a more global and cosmic perspective, for you are under the process which quickens. Let us speak of the influence of cosmic bodies such as the sun and the moon. You are used to the ancient science of astrology as well, which has atrophied in its attention similar to your own sensory abilities. Like electrons, they orbit along their paths with an essence and energy of their being and in so doing resonate or ring their unique vibrations that emanate from them. For example, you are used to understanding the moon and its gravitational and emotional pull or influence. It is both a physical and mental influence on energies of matter and non-matter, or consciousness."

"It would be as a ball that is swung on a string by another and as it is swung near your ears, the vibration of it becomes louder, the vibration of it entraining with specific parts of you that are receptive to it—like your chakras in particular. All cosmic bodies and things create different resonances of vibration and have different unique purposes that are projected, affecting Gaia and all living things to some degree. This becomes more or

less intense depending upon its distance, alignment with others, and position, like several swinging balls. Their individual and joint vibrations that emanate can affect your consciousness which is itself energy in a wave form and indeed through the chakras that link the physical body to affect biochemistry and behaviour. It is all interacting energies."

"There are many, many such cycles and influences of this nature that come and go and combine into different patterns, setting a environment for all living things and some of these are very long indeed. .All cosmic things have characteristics of vibration like you and emit these in the form of waves which is what all that is, is. You do the same with your own heart field and your unique signatures. The effect of course is different on each that receives it or comes under the influence. Other characteristics such as heat, ultraviolet, infrared, and special cosmic particles of energy are felt by you and known by your science but the characteristics of love, or compassion or spirit are not so obvious to you. They are nevertheless the same, emanating as wave vibrations upon the bodies and minds of all living energies, in different ways or intensities depending upon the vibrational or resonant makeup of each."

"We tell you this because it is important to understand there are influences and energies at play here that are all interacting to contribute to the overall influence of consciousness on your planet, irrespective of whether these are 3D, 4D, or 5D states. Such cycles and alignments affect your seasons, your growth and expansion of all living things."

"This knowledge of the star systems and the cosmic influences were handed down from ancient knowledge to many who have retained it in some form. The Mayans are more known but this is also written and known in other continents with the Tibetans, Egyptians, American

Indians, and many others. The Mayans were very knowledgeable and understood the workings as related to their growing seasons and life within it. They were conscious of the influences and knew of the longer cycles and alignments of cosmic forces. Thus they indeed knew of the point of 2012 as the time when the shift to a new age would occur from material time to no time—a time when the overall resonance would reach a zenith and a shift into a new consciousness would be complete."

"This has to do with the ascension of Gaia and those symbiant to her. It involves the influence of vibrations that flood her and you from cosmic neighbours and from her own larger living body of which she is but a part. These cosmic influences and cycles are vibrations that are influencing the ascension and these are of a nature that you have not yet understood, such as the energy of love and of unity, of spirit and wholeness, of the Light of the Creator—the One. It is of the rising of love and the higher energies that set the scene and the background to Gaia's movie being played out. And as you are symbiant to her, as One, you are all influenced to some degree."

"As Gaia moves into her galactic alignment which is a cycle of 26000 of your years, it moves into a large portion of an intergalactic cycle of 12 times that. And as it approached the zenith of the influence, the influence and hence the pace of potential change quickens as the resonance strengthens. The influence of the bodies, their characteristics and their unique emanations increase as the alignment approaches where a maximum is reached, then a new setting like a new scene in a movie begins to take over and the old fades. It is cycles of the new age of influence of Aquarius. This is not an instant process. It is strengthening and weakening of vibrational influence, like the pull of the moon on your oceans—and your consciousness. Your event of a full moon is but an event

as noted in your time for example; but the changes in its influence are a gradual, natural process."

"As individual units of consciousness and energetic bodies, you have your own vibrational signatures that entrain with the larger settings and bodies in different degrees and different specific affects—but yet all the same in a larger overall scope."

"This now is a point where the influences and alignments quicken as the zenith of many influences combine in a unique configuration. It is the 2012 time—yes where the zenith is reached and point of greatest influence upon Gaia and her living things is created. It is important to understand that this process has already been occurring. And all is affected to some degree but you have free will as the creator beings of Light to choose the path and the degree to which you accept the influence, and the direction it points to. Not all will ascend with Gaia and live out their lives according to the energies they create. She like many other creatures does not have the option. Even though the influences and the body changes to your consciousness come to your awareness, this does not mean that all will choose the higher path."

"As the process intensifies, as understood by the Mayans, a final cycle of ascension and expansion comes into influence, going through its 13 periods within the one year 2011. This is concurrent with all other major cycles that complete their process together at the same point and hence this was stated as the time of no time— the time when the spiritual essence of the One would prevail and complete the shift of consciousness. As we have told you, the new spiritual parallel world being formed by those that are choosing the higher path is a result of this influence and shift in consciousness. It will become a world of as above—as formed in the Higher Divine Minds—to the so below of a new reality for those that have seen, and are of the Light."

"As we have stated before, this is a transition of energy movement and influences, a phasing as energies entrain and shift. It is not an event of instant change and catastrophe as some would like to instil as a point of fear and destruction. It is so that the nature of the ones that remain on the Lower Path and their influence on consciousness, hence Gaia's reaction, can be seen as abrupt reactions upon her much like has been so in the past. But we must say that the power of these who choose dominion and control is waning as the ascension vibrations quicken and the energy of truth and peace gains momentum."

"The process is one of a graceful transition and evolution into a new spiritual age of enlightenment and expansion, not of fear and destruction. You know now your place in this movie and that you are an eternal being. You know your hologram of perfection, and that your parallel world is indeed real and awaits your choice of how and when you enter it. It will become increasingly real to you on the upper path, especially as you learn to walk both. As the drama unfolds in the lower path and the 3D hologram, it is the larger consciousness that will determine how the transition of the 3D world hologram is expressed in its material form. How this unfolds is partly influenced by those who choose dominion over others and how their influence overrides the new consciousness influence from above—and those that are of the Light."

"It is Gaia's time to ascend and move into her rightful place as it is yours. It is a process that is set in the Mind of God and its cosmic workings. As it is all One, you are part of the ascension process as is all else. But the choices each individual conscious being makes, and the path chosen, and the way it is to unfold into the life that is completed upon Gaia is not decided. It is each that must choose."

The Great Convergence

"For now we will complete our message of ascension. For this you will remember the sessions on Parallel Worlds. These are indeed the Upper and Lower Paths of the ascension choices that unfold before you all. Both paths receive the same amount of Light of the One and the ascension energy of awakening. It is all equal but the attention and the awareness to it is very different. As Gaia ascends her own physical body changes as her Higher Essence draws the lower form upwards into the light. This will mean, like your own body, that the body will lighten and begin to change its properties as well."

"As this proceeds, towards the Grand Alignment within the Galactic system of 2012, and the alignment of Gaia's heart with others and the Galactic center of heart known as the center of the Milky Way, the characteristics change and reach the zenith, shifting like in you and those energies that are not aligned with this fade and dissolve away, transmuted into the dominant energy of the Light and Love of the Source. Those energies that are not compatible will change and shift upon Gaia and the consciousness of humanity that enfolds her. Just as lower forms of energy do not exist in the higher realms, so it is with the negative and darker energies of control, dominion and conflict. The essence moves to the central heart of the Galaxy and aligns. These lower energies lose their strength as attention to the new shifts and the awareness and attention increases."

"At the same time, Gaia's properties shift in terms of her physical nature, affecting weather, temperature, water, air, and she begins to glow and shine within her larger body and her scope within the universe expands. Many old energies and devices and material things will begin to be dysfunctional and irrelevant, not supported by the old ways. These will be replaced by the new, more in

alignment with the consciousness of the One and all being in harmony with her. These new ways and energies are already surrounding Gaia."

"As the consciousness opens and cosmic neighbours open to the new awareness, new discoveries, processes compatible with Gaia's changing body will be embraced and brought forward as many are ready to meet this calling and many are ready to lead and show the new way. The Crystal Children will awaken and emerge to take their rightful place as they will feel the draw with a deepness and strength that will bewilder those that are not awakened. They will teach their knowing and their advanced abilities as will the ones of the Higher Path are learning and doing. As this process evolves and quickens towards the alignment of galactic hearts with the heart of One, many changes will occur. The old energy of polarity will fade and a new leader will emerge under the command of their Higher Divine Selves."

"This will reflect the convergence of the higher parallel world of perfection and the lower evolving world of Gaia into One. It is those on the Higher Path that will unfold this which will reach its zenith in 2012 and the alignment with the Galactic Heart. It is how the two worlds are walked."

"Now you walk in the 3D world and are learning to walk differently in your Higher World. This is not yet congealed but has formed through the joint consciousness of those who are awakened and increasing in numbers rapidly, having chosen the Upper Path. What you and many others are doing now is learning to walk both paths as you are spending more of your linear time here. In fact, you are here always but you have not learned to bring the real essence of your physical body here yet. This world that you see clearly now has no limits and it is the learning of bringing the heavier body to the higher realm that is your attention

now. As below, the way of it is to have the Higher Mind and Body brought consciously to live upon Gaia and bring limitless possibilities to her and your family which is all that is One. Over time a convergence of this will occur. This is the ascension."

"Through this immediate period there will be those that sleep or resist, who will not awaken, as there are those that will work to impede the ascension as it does not serve their cause. Yet these are ones who have a heart but is semi disconnected since they protect and love their own kind. They have become subservient to their needs of power and their DNA is dominant here. The conflict of this dark and light will become resolved as more and more light shines upon you, Gaia, and them. You have learned in your Higher Path of the Divine Mind that you indeed have an advantage and the choice to help open the hearts of these beings. Even within their own world, they are filled with fear and conflict of loss and dear ones, and in the wake of the consciousness shift, and the dissolving of the power energies they use, there is indeed a crack in their beings that leads to the heart. Yes, it means working in your perfect world above—in your mind now but in a firmer more physical reality later, bringing above to below and below to above as it was meant to be."

"As these energy forces clash, as they are so now, over the next years the strain of polarity will be felt, both on Gaia and her living things and this will also reach its zenith, but the wake is one of underlying fading of dark energy strength and the light energy strengthening. During this period it is important to understand that the dark ones are attempting to take desperate means to counteract and to confuse this new consciousness, using devices, technology and their knowledge of the higher worlds so as to flood dysfunction and generate lower energies as Gaia shifts. It is important to transmute such

energy for it can find expression upon Gaia depending on the strength and determination of it."

"It is this scene that has evolved and is evolving. And it is this that will affect the nature of the lower physical world and how it remains in its new state of ascension. We under cosmic law cannot interfere with this process but you now understand that you can. The process of working in the upper dimensions is awakening in you and you are becoming aware of yourself and what you can do here. As you learn and do by your attention and intent, it is important to remain grounded to Gaia—to your 3D world through your nine chakras so as to balance above and below—Heaven and Earth. The top Heaven chakra will keep you connected to Source and the heart will balance."

"Through the confusion of energy change, you need to understand that as the new consciousness grows and floods Gaia, the old fades, one replacing the other. Together these energies of conscious purpose and type create the whole of the influences of consciousness. As one fades, the new replaces and as the new increases to the zenith at the Grand Galactic Heart alignment, all of the old will be replaced. As this proceeds, your crystalline structure will slowly move you away from the usual 3D body requirements especially any that are not aligned with the Higher Divine mind and heart. This is the Higher Path you have chosen."

"The energies remaining will become foreign such as the lizard energies that are within your DNA. For many, as with you, this has changed as it is the awareness of it that allows you to eliminate the influence of it and to begin the atrophy process from your DNA and the filling of your DNA with the light of the One—your true spiritual essence. But it is important that this awareness come into the consciousness, for if it does not, as you know these beings have learned to open and activate these

lower negative energies in your DNA from the upper dimension. The draw of this Lizard DNA will become less and less in many as the body slowly changes from the flood of ascension energies. However, your Divine platform, as we have stated, places you in a higher plane of more light from where you can also do your work with them."

"What will evolve of your 3D world is yet to be written as the desperate ones and their choices are yet to be made. We do know however, that those on the Higher Path are indeed shifting the balance rapidly—so rapid now that much attention is upon this tiny little planet of Earth and her little Creators."

It seems the lower path tells me
I am a man dreaming of a better me
But the higher path says that's a scam
A better me dreams I am a man

What path is it you decide to take?
To bring a Higher or Lower fate
The time is nigh to make a choice
Mine is One Love, One Voice

When you find yourself within
You know in your heart there is no sin
And everything that you need to know
Opens up to you with love's flow

BEGIN
END

And now we come to the final bit
There seems no way of stopping it
Ascension has its own life you know
The Lower Path I must let go

So how does one learn to Let Go? Let me bring back some trite statements I brought forward at the start of the book. These were on suggestions on how to execute the paradigm shift on creating miracles and *doing the right thing*:

You: *"How do you know this is right?"*
Me: *"I just do."*
You: *"How do you create the right attention?"*
Me: *"By bringing something into your mind."*
You: *"How do you go inside to the Heart?"*
Me: *"Anyway you like or just say it to be so."*
You: *"How do you detach from the outcome?"*
Me: *"Stop thinking."*
You: *"How do you zero out your intellect?"*
Me: *"Trust there is guidance from the heart."*
You: *"How do you vibrate with desire?"*
Me: *"Feel the bliss of being perfect."*
You: *"How do you believe without doubt?"*
Me: *"Because it simply is."*
You: *"Is there a specific procedure?"*
Me: *"No, it is what works for you."*
You: *"So how do you know you are doing it properly?"*
Me: *"When it works."*

You: *"Well how long will that take?"*
Me: *"As long as you take."*
You: *"Anything else?"*
Me: *"Yes, use the words I love you a lot!"*

Does this make more sense now? It's when you believe **you** are holding the power of Divine Love within your heart and there is really no one else or anything but you in the way. How long will that take? It's how long you take to believe in it and live it. Do you think you have anything to lose? I think not. Is it difficult? If you can't forgive and let go of that which is painful, it is. If you think love has conditions, it is. If you believe what science tells you, it is.

I want to end this book with a few summaries on Letting Go. This comes from some very wondrous Light Workers on planet Earth. To them practicing miracles, doing incredible psychic work, doing wondrous energy and grid healing, and teaching the higher realm of metaphysics is just old hat. These are people who are on the Let Go side of the vibrational stages. They have learned to "Let Go" and they have some advice.

Morganne Rayne

Before 'letting go' there is attachment;
    Inherent in attachment is suffering.
After 'letting go' there is heaven;
    Inherent in heaven is Love.

Realizing what you are attached to is easy,
    Follow your suffering.
Realizing you are in Love is easy,
    Follow your heart.

Detach now.

The Bridge to Heaven is 'letting go'.

Denny Underwood

"You must become as a child. Become, Believe, and Trust as a child."

"What does this mean? It means that a child's belief system is not based on the biases of others beliefs. Their belief systems are pure and totally uncorrupted by the input or belief systems of others. They have no bias, no preconceived notions. A child's beliefs are based solely on the quintessence of Pure Love and trust. THIS is the very same Love that formed the Universe. If you say to a child of 2 or 3 that clouds are the pillows, where Angels are sleeping, they will not argue with you, they believe and trust that what you are telling them is truth. They are innocent to any corruption, opinions, or falsehoods."

"So then, we must become as a child with the innocence and full faith, trust, and unconditional love that a child possesses. For once we allow ourselves to become a child; we then begin to live within the Highest Unconditional Love Vibration that is our true selves, thereby touching others in the unconditional love consciousness that connects us all."

Kenneth Walter

"To me, to Let Go is to create bliss. The ultimate of goals of letting go is to be true to 'THE' and appear clear before infinity Creation/Creator."

"Ground one's self through the Earth Chakra to rid the mind of chatter, emotional sensations and any

physical pain. Drain your Chakra channels to Let Go of all stagnant energy through your entire body and realms of bodies through the Earth Chakra. By doing so you will find the place that feels like the purest essence of TRUE Beauty. This is letting go; uniting with the universal flow that permeates all; a point of stillness where you will find the deep and profound sense of AAAhhhhhhhhhhh."

"Clarity IS given by letting go, I have found this simple process described here to lead to blissful states of peace and cosmic alignment."

"Let Go and Let Flow"

Beverly Michaluk

"Most people can look back over the years and identify a time and place at which their lives changed significantly. Whether by accident or design, these are the moments when, because of a readiness within us and a collaboration with events occurring around us, we are forced to seriously reappraise ourselves and the conditions under which we live and to make certain choices that will affect the rest of our lives. Letting go will only allow you to see what gift the universe has in store for you."

Mark Sorenson

"Put your intellect in a box, attach a pair of wings to it, and watch it fly away. Get out of your head and into your heart."

And finally...

I have taken the Upper Path and things are unfolding rapidly, as they are on Planet Earth and its older energies. I will be reporting my progress on the Upper Path. If you have understood about Letting Go, enjoy your ride and hold on!

So what is it that means "to be"
Am I not already me?
Well it all depends on who you hear
It's your Lower Self that speaks my Dear

About two of you, you may not know
You have made that clear so how
Can you not listen to your Higher Self?
And put your Lower on the shelf

It's easy if you stop the do
And be the Higher One you were meant to
Be in your heart all your day
Your Lower Self will fade away

When you really let go and be
You are again Divine eternity
There is nothing you really have to do
But be the Love that is really you

Ed Rychkun

www.ingramcontent.com/pod-product-compliance
Lightning Source LLC
Chambersburg PA
CBHW060518100426
42743CB00009B/1367